THE HEALING WAY

About the author:
Kristin A. Kunzman, M.A., is a licensed psychologist in private practice in Minneapolis. She specializes in working with women, couples, and families recovering from childhood sexual abuse and alcoholism. She also conducts workshops on sexuality, abuse, and self-esteem.

THE HEALING WAY

Adult Recovery from Childhood Sexual Abuse

Kristin A. Kunzman

First published June 1990.

ISBN: 0-89486-663-X

Library of Congress Catalog Card Number: 90-80389

Printed in the United States of America.

Editor's note:
Hazelden Educational Materials offers a variety of information on chemical dependency and related areas. Our publications do not necessarily represent Hazelden or its programs, nor do they officially speak for any Twelve Step organization.

The stories in this book are composites of many individuals. Any similarity to any one person is purely coincidental.

To the survivors, in hopes that their courage to work through the pain of the past, and their commitment to healing themselves in the present, will help create a more loving future for children everywhere.

CONTENTS

PREFACE

In the mid-to-late 1970s, I worked at a community agency counseling chemically dependent women both before and after they went through chemical dependency treatment. At this time, I had already been through such treatment myself and was involved in a Twelve Step recovery group to help me stay sober. I found myself struck by how difficult staying sober was for many of my clients. I therefore set out to learn why recovery from chemical dependency was harder for some women than for others.

I focused attention on and asked more questions of the women who were having the most difficulty with sobriety. It turned out that many of them had been victims* of childhood sexual abuse. Over a decade ago, women in chemical dependency treatment were generally not asked about past sexual abuse, which meant the abuse was not acknowledged or talked about in treatment, and women leaving treatment were not aware the abuse may have contributed to their chemical dependency and that they might need to get some help for it. This seems to be changing, and chemical dependency professionals are becoming more aware of and sensitive to women who have been abused sexually.

In 1978, I developed and began administering an agency program for helping female children, adolescents, and women with histories of sexual abuse. In the beginning, most of the adult women I saw were chemically dependent. That base of clients, however, grew to include many women who were not chemically dependent, but who had developed a wide variety of other physical, psychological, and emotional problems stemming from sexual abuse. Through this work,

---

* *Victim* seems the better term when referring to a child, but adult survivor seems appropriate for women with a background of being sexually abused as children or teens.

I realized how profoundly adult survivors are influenced and entrapped by unspoken secrets and buried negative feelings surrounding their abuse. It affects almost every aspect of their adult lives. In order for abuse survivors to rebuild fulfilling lives for themselves today and in the future, it's important for them to uncover, understand, and conquer their past memories.

In the years since I began working with women with histories of sexual abuse, friends have asked if it's depressing to work with people who have had such "horrifying" and "painful" things done to them. I can honestly answer no, because adult survivors attempting to reclaim their lives are amazing women. Their courage in facing their painful pasts and their dedication to making their lives into something better is awe-inspiring. It's humbling and rewarding to watch these women put the pieces of their lives back together in group and individual therapy. It's exciting to see them go on to explore the expanded horizons of their newfound strengths and abilities.

In the past decade there have been some major changes for the better regarding recognition and treatment of sexual abuse and its effects. I hope this book will, in some small part, add to the growing body of work that is trying to help adult survivors overcome the effects of the sexual abuse they suffered as children and let them go on to lead fulfilling and productive lives.

Thanks are due to Mary Froiland — co-therapist, best of friends, and an important teacher — as a major influence on my thinking and this book. Thanks also to all the other dedicated and talented professionals I have had the pleasure of working with and learning from over the years, including Barb Olson, Wendy Farrar, Kathleen Kunzman, and Reneé Faucher for valuable criticisms of the work in progress, and Pat Boland for her editing expertise and for believing the book was worth publishing.

A heartfelt red pencil salute to my husband, J. Gillespie, who read all these words more than once and encouraged me to keep on writing. Special inspiration was supplied by my daughters, Rickie and Ellie, whose boundless energy and joy in living constantly renew my faith that a good life is worth fighting for.

INTRODUCTION

Are you one of the approximately one out of three women who was sexually abused as a child or teenager? This question is difficult for many adult survivors of childhood sexual abuse to answer. While some survivors may remember every aspect of their abuse with alarming clarity, others repress it so thoroughly that no conscious memory of it survives, except perhaps as vague dream images or recurrent nightmares.

Sexual abuse of children cuts across all boundaries of class, race, religion, education, and economic status. All of us, whether we know it or not, come into daily contact with survivors of such abuse: relatives, friends, neighbors, co-workers, or fellow church members. There is also a growing recognition that the number of male children abused is much greater than previously thought, and many of the problems stemming from that abuse, and the methods for healing from it, are the same for both men and women. But there are differences, and since my knowledge comes from working with women, this book is addressed to them.

Why are so many children abused? It's a complex mixture of cultural and family dynamics that is really just beginning to be understood. This book doesn't have the answers for all the "whys" behind the sexual abuse of children. The important thing to understand is that it happens much too often. And it happens to innocent children and teenagers who don't understand what is going on — except that they feel betrayed, unloved, unprotected, and alone.

Four major ways in which childhood sexual abuse affects survivors are:

- It disturbs and distorts feelings over developing bodies and sexuality.
- It violates personal rights and creates feelings of powerlessness, hopelessness, and shame.

- It damages the ability to develop feelings of trust toward others.
- It passes on a family blueprint of undernurturing and inconsistent care for the next generation.

If you are an adult survivor, an important thing for you to understand and believe at some point in your healing process is that you were not responsible for the abuse you suffered as a child or teenager. It's not unusual if you don't believe that right now. When children are abused, one of the ways they try to make sense of the abuse or preserve the belief that the abuser is someone they can still trust (especially if the abuser is a parent) is to tell themselves the abuse happened because they were bad. This sense of inner badness will gradually go away as you learn more about the abuse and understand that children and teen victims can be easily manipulated or coerced by an older, more powerful abuser.

I wrote this book to be used as a beginning guide, in addition to the help offered through therapy or support groups, to give survivors a road map for their journey to recovery. You will also find courage and strength in the continuing struggles of other adult survivors — their examples can help you discover your own strong points and special survival skills. It really is possible to change what feels like a hopeless life into a hope-filled one.

My hope is that this book will help you discover healthy and effective ways of moving beyond your painful past. I hope that you will come to care about yourself and be cared about by others in ways that you may never have experienced in your family. I would also hope that you can learn to enjoy your sexuality without being plagued by flashbacks, shame, and other problems that negatively affect your life as a sexual person. By learning how to discover and fully use your considerable inner resources, you can begin living the kind of integrated, empowered, and fulfilling life you are capable of living.

CHAPTER ONE

WHAT IS CHILDHOOD SEXUAL ABUSE?

Many women with questions concerning childhood sexual abuse have a difficult time deciding if they were really abused or not. Minimizing, denial, and poor definitions of what childhood sexual abuse is may make it difficult for them to identify the abuse in their past. For example, a woman came into therapy complaining of feeling "bad" about herself. She didn't trust people, she had difficulty having close relationships, and she felt hopeless and depressed much of the time. In general, she felt as if a black cloud was perpetually hanging over her. While she was unable to pinpoint where her feelings came from, she knew something was wrong.

She revealed that she was verbally abused and emotionally neglected by both her parents during childhood. She said that as a teen, she had felt "like a prostitute" when her father stared at her body and made "joking" comments about what a sexy young thing she was — that maybe he better get her a chastity belt. He showed her pictures of naked women in his *Playboy* magazine and said maybe someday her breasts would get big enough to get her in there.

She was embarrassed and hurt by his comments then, and yet she remembered those conversations as the times he was nicest to her. She had very mixed feelings about those interactions.

Even with all this evidence, she had great difficulty accepting the fact that her family system was abusive and undernurturing. It was also hard for her to accept that her father's sexual comments and showing pornography to her for his pleasure was sexually abusive. She tried to minimize and deny her experiences: "Oh, it really wasn't that bad, I guess. . . ." Since what happened to her didn't include sexual intercourse, threats, or physical force, it couldn't, in her eyes, be called sexual abuse.

This sort of denial is common in adult survivors of childhood abuse. Becoming aware of the denial is the beginning of a gradual process of realization that many survivors go through in order to deal with the pain. One of the most important things survivors need to learn is that sexual abuse appears in many forms other than intercourse. Another important thing for survivors to learn is that children and teenagers aren't in an equal relationship with adults — that means it is the adult's responsibility to provide a safe environment for the child or teen. Children and teenagers, then, are not responsible for sexual abuse inflicted on them.

CHILDHOOD SEXUAL ABUSE HAS MANY FORMS

Childhood sexual abuse is a physical violation of a child's body through any sort of sexual contact or a psychological violation of the child through verbal or nonverbal sexual behavior. It is neglectful, disrespectful, and hurtful because it violates a child's basic rights to be protected, nurtured, and guided through childhood.

Sexual abuse of children happens in various ways, some of which may be overlooked and discounted. Childhood sexual abuse covers a wide range of behavior from covert episodes such as a father staring at his daughter's breasts

2

and saying, "You're really pretty. It's too bad your breasts are so small," to the overt action of an older brother raping his preteen sister over a period of years.

The three things that seem to most affect the degree of hurt resulting from sexual abuse are:

1. How close the relationship is between the abuser and the child victim. The closer the relationship, the more damage seems to be caused.
2. Whether the abuser is an adult or another child. The greater the age difference, the more hurtful are some long-term effects.
3. The level of violence or cruelty involved. The more violent or cruel the abuse, the greater the consequences.

Overt and Covert Sexual Abuse— Both Take a Heavy Toll on Victims

The following list describes some ways children are abused by adults. The adult

- allows the child no privacy for bathing or dressing.
- is obsessed with the child's genitals and bodily functions; stares at the child's genitals.
- fondles the child.
- makes repeated remarks and is preoccupied over the child's developing body.
- shows the child pornography.
- French kisses the child.
- exposes his genitals to the child.
- gives the child excessive enemas or is excessive about genital hygiene.
- has oral sex with the child.
- practices sodomy with the child.
- has intercourse with the child.

The majority of sexual abuse does *not* take the form of intercourse. Other physical and nonphysical forms are much more common, including the following examples:

- *Fondling and masturbation.* Either done by an adult to the child or vice versa.
- *Inappropriate sleeping arrangements.* For example, the child sleeps with her grandfather while grandmother sleeps down the hall. Or this may involve a much younger sibling who sleeps in the same bed with an older sibling of a different sex. This puts the child in a vulnerable situation where physical forms of sexual abuse may occur.
- *Sexual jokes and graphic sexual descriptions.* When told to children, these are a form of verbal pornography and are really said to provide sexual pleasure for the adult who tells them.
- *Inappropriate and unwanted hugs, kisses, and tickling.* If you've ever been tickled far beyond the point of asking for it to stop, you know the anger and fear this behavior causes. Sometimes, this tickling feels sexual or uncomfortable, even though it looks innocent. Trust your feelings that it may not have been intended innocently. "Innocent" tickling and hugs can cross the line into sexual abuse, often resulting in "accidental" touching of genitals or prolonged kissing.

The fact is that any type of childhood sexual abuse, no matter how covert it is and how "harmless" the abuser portrays it, can have far-reaching and destructive consequences to the victim. The following story of an adult survivor is typical of the type of covert sexual abuse that happens to many children.

> *My dad never touched me, but I never felt safe around him anyway. He was a surgeon and worked long hours, so as kids we always had to be quiet when he was home, and even then he always seemed to be on edge. I always felt my dad was staring at me and*

4

spying on me when I dressed and when I wore a bathing suit. Nothing I could really put my finger on, but something always felt creepy. He always had some excuse for coming into our rooms or the bathroom when we were dressing. We had no privacy at all. When he drank, which was frequently, he was friendlier and more seductive toward me. I was very self-conscious about my body as a young girl and teenager. My dad teased me for wearing baggy clothes that hid my body. He said I would never catch a guy if I didn't show off my "wares." I started to feel very ugly around this time and started making myself throw up before school so I would look thinner. I thought if I didn't look so filled out maybe my dad would stop saying those things to me.

Notice how the woman telling the story blames herself for her father's abusive behavior toward her. Obviously, it wasn't her fault. Many adult survivors tried to physically change their bodies to mask their emerging sexuality as children or adolescents. Such behavior may set off a lifelong pattern of either anorexic starvation, bulimia, or other eating disorders.

The more overt forms of childhood sexual abuse — mutual masturbation, intercourse, and oral sex — are what most people think of when childhood sexual abuse is mentioned. It's easy to understand the physical and psychological pain a child feels who has had intercourse or oral sex with an adult. It is more difficult to grasp the damage of a continual stream of sexual comments of an adult to a child. Both types of abuse take a heavy toll on the victims.

No matter what form it takes, childhood sexual abuse causes great and long-lasting hurt to its victims.

Did anyone ever touch your genitals or have you touch theirs?

Were you ever French kissed or sexually penetrated in any way?

Were you subject to embarrassing and degrading sexual remarks and taunts?

Were you spied on while dressing or bathing?

Were you given excessive enemas or were your genitals frequently and harshly washed because you were always "dirty"?

Were you shown sexual pictures or invited to watch X-rated videos?

It doesn't matter whether the abuse was physical or non-physical, verbal or visual. Sexual abuse interrupts childhood learning at several crucial stages and contributes to the development of low self-esteem, distorted beliefs about body image and sexuality, and a lack of trust in caregivers and the world in general. If you were forced or coerced into or exposed to any sort of sexual contact — physical or non-physical — as a child or teenager, you were sexually abused.

WHO ARE THE ABUSERS?

There is a common myth that childhood sexual abuse is usually committed by a stranger — a "pervert" — attacking a child on the street. But, in fact, the vast majority of childhood sexual abuse is done by family members, friends of the family, or authority figures known to the child, such as teachers, ministers, or neighbors. For that reason, this book deals primarily with the first three categories of abusers — relatives, family friends, and authority figures. This doesn't discount the pain and horror of abuse involving strangers, but in some very important ways the long-term psychological damage may not be as great since issues of trust, love, and enforced secrecy aren't involved. This, of course, assumes that victims of strangers can tell parents and receive counseling and are from nurturing families.

Incest

Sexual abuse where both the abuser and the victim are related is *incestuous*. Incest refers to sexual relations between relatives other than a husband and wife (who are not otherwise related). Other forms of sexual abuse taking place between relatives — such as sexual remarks or the use of pornography — that don't involve intercourse or other physical contact may also be termed incestuous.

All sexual abuse is hurtful to children.* But the effects of incestuous sexual abuse may be even more devastating because of the added sense of betrayal and abandonment caused by the abuse taking place within the family — the one place where children *should* feel the safest.

THE PSYCHOLOGICAL DAMAGE OF CHILDHOOD SEXUAL ABUSE

The psychological damage resulting from childhood sexual abuse may be many times more hurtful than the physical pain or humiliation suffered during abusive episodes. Most adult survivors feel *they* were responsible for the abuse. The fact that the abuse is commonly done by someone the child knows and trusts reinforces this feeling and contributes to the enormity and depth of the trauma he or she feels. It is especially damaging because children need consistent safety and trust to feel secure. Thus, the abuse by someone close to them violates a basic need that they be cared for and watched over by their parents and family.

Isolation

Children sexually abused by a family member feel isolated because, in most cases, they feel there is no one they can

---

* From this point on, I will use the word *children* to refer to both children and teenagers.

7

safely tell about the abuse. They have been treated as objects and as adults; they have been included in adult behavior: an older person has imposed a behavior beyond their level of learning and experience and contrary to their well-being. The sexual abuse may not always hurt physically, but since it involves coercion, confusion, manipulation, and betrayal, it is devastating emotionally.

Threats and Secrets

Abused children are almost always physically or emotionally threatened by their perpetrators. Common threats include beatings, death, parental hatred, jail, and the withdrawal of affection and approval. These are devastating thoughts for children who already suffer emotionally from a lack of parental nurturing. Abusers and other family members sometimes argue that the abused child "wanted" or "asked" for the sexual abuse. No matter how "loving" or "willing" a perpetrator may try to color it, sexual abuse always involves the abuser's power to coerce the child against his or her will.

To make matters worse, the abuse is almost always treated as a secret — a terrible secret that children must bear alone. Caught up in a "dirty little secret" with the perpetrator, the children feel shame and guilt. As one survivor put it:

My stepbrother used to come into my room late at night when he came home from work. He always smelled of whiskey or beer, and he made me be sexual with him. I knew it was wrong, but I didn't know how to stop it. I was only seven when it first happened, and he told me to keep it a secret. He said if my mom ever found out she would put me in an orphanage, a place where they sent all the "bad little girls." My mom was kind of out of it, I guess. She never seemed to suspect anything was wrong. It kept happening until I was ten, but then he went into the army and was killed in Vietnam. I remember feeling happy about that, but I ended up feeling guilty about that too! I carried the secret around with me for twenty years; it was eating away at me all that time. What a waste.

For most adult survivors, the combination of the sexual abuse, the secrecy surrounding it, and the incredible isolation and shame they feel as a result continues to cause great stress. It colors their present-day life. Breaking through the wall of secrecy is a first and most important step to recovery.

If you find yourself trying to explain to someone your secret of what it felt like to be a sexual abuse victim, try using this analogy: Ask that person to imagine being forced to do something he or she doesn't want to do. Suggest something scary that the person doesn't understand, that he or she somehow knows is very wrong — for example, robbing a store. Someone the person trusts is saying, "If you don't rob the store with me and keep it a secret, you or someone you love will be badly hurt." The stress and tension of such a situation, a no-win situation, would be tremendous. This may help people understand the stress and conflict you have felt.

It is no wonder that in many cases, the ordeal of living in an abusive situation parallels the experiences of hostages and concentration camp prisoners who suffer post-traumatic stress disorders. Living it for one day would be an ordeal, but spending a childhood that way is devastating. It is no wonder that psychological damages inflicted by such trauma are carried into adulthood.

Post-Traumatic Stress Disorder

Post-traumatic stress disorder is a label or diagnosis given to the condition suffered by people who lived through a traumatic event in their lives. They emotionally and mentally reexperience all or part of the event's stress at unpredictable moments and in unpredictable ways. You may have seen stories about this in regard to Vietnam veterans. The constant strain of combat conditions — needing to be ever alert and wary and being uncertain who was the enemy and who was a friend — caused some soldiers so much psychological stress they continued to feel the effects twenty or more years later. They experienced flashbacks (a memory of a traumatic event), and in extreme cases, they confused people in the present with enemies from the past.

It's not surprising that many of these same effects appear in adult survivors of childhood sexual abuse. After all, they were under constant strain, wondering when the next abusive attack would come, and there was the same sort of confusion over who was friend and foe. Combat veterans and sexual abuse victims alike may turn to alcohol and other drugs to dull their painful feelings and memories.

Neglect and Abandonment

The neglect that is part of growing up in a sexually abusive family causes the children to feel abandoned. They constantly fear for their well-being and perhaps even for their lives. It isn't just the abuse itself that causes the traumatic stress, but the coercion, the threats, the secrets, the guilt, and the constant fear and dread of discovery and punishment. All these feelings are coupled with the most horrible reality of all: the people who are supposed to be caring for the child fail to do their job. This lack of consistent, protective love and nurturing by the primary caregivers — the parents — hurts most of all.

What happens when sexually abused children finally escape the family circle or the abuse is stopped? Unless something is done to change the incredibly strong and enduring negative feelings from their childhood, they will carry these feelings with them wherever they go, and the emotional trauma will darken their adult years as it did their childhoods. It may be present as nightmares, flashbacks, fleeting memories, and intrusive waking thoughts. Feelings and memories may be buried for years, but they are not buried forever. Unless survivors take positive steps to deal with their feelings by sharing them with someone they trust, these feelings will continue to resurface and terrorize their adult lives. This is called *retraumatization.*

Retraumatization of the Survivor

Retraumatization occurs when an event triggers memories, actions, or feelings that recall part or all of the original traumatic experience (triggers can be a particular place, smell, or touch). Thus, if a sexually abused person doesn't "work through" or come to terms with her abuse in some way, certain authority figures, a mate, male sexuality (especially if it mimics in some way the type of abuse suffered), certain sights, smells, or sounds — can trigger a vast assortment of negative feelings connected with the original abuse.

Some signs of retraumatization are

- intense emotional pain or grief,
- anxiety attacks,
- fear of approaching certain people,
- flashbacks to the previous trauma,
- regular nightmares,
- compulsive or phobic behavior,
- feelings of terror, and
- severe isolation.

There are things you can do to avoid retraumatization besides avoiding your trigger mechanisms. This involves putting the memory pieces together into real events instead of the nightmarish fragments. We will discuss these methods more fully in Chapter Four.

SOME AFTEREFFECTS OF ABUSE

As adults, women who were abused develop ways of coping with the aftereffects of the trauma. What follows is a list of these aftereffects, with quotes from adult survivors who describe their feelings and behaviors resulting from the aftereffects.

Intense Shame and Low Self-Esteem

I felt shameful and guilty about what happened, because I thought somehow it must be all my fault. When you're a part of something that is secret and wrong, you feel wrong inside.

Isolation from Others

I felt so alone when I was growing up. I was shy, but I also felt unacceptable. I wanted so badly to join in, but instead I sat alone and the others made fun of me. As an adult, I've learned to at least fake joining in, but I feel the same as I did when I was a kid: alone and not good enough.

Difficulty Trusting Others

I grew up with the idea that blood is thicker than water. But if my own family didn't love me enough to stop abusing me, how can I expect others to? I'm trying to change that.

Lack of Rights and Privacy

I know now that I grew up being violated in important ways, like my mom would always barge into my room without knocking when I was getting dressed. She would even come into the bathroom when I was showering and start a fight with me while I was standing there naked. But it's still hard to know when someone is taking advantage of me, and to know when I have the right to say no. I swing from being passive to being over-reactive, with little middle ground.

Confusion of Sex and Affection

I felt invisible in my family most of the time. The only times I ever felt I was noticed or got any attention was when my stepdad would look at me, in this creepy way he had, and make comments about my body and say stuff like he wanted to see what was growing under my sweater: Kleenex or tits. And like that was supposed to be a joke or something. It felt icky to me, but at the same time it often seemed better than being totally ignored.

Confusing Lovers with Perpetrators (Flashbacks)

My sexual relationships always seem to go fine at the beginning: we're getting along, having fun, the sex is great. Then, all of a sudden, I feel as if my dad is right there touching me. I feel so crazy that I usually have an anxiety attack and think that I'm going nuts. I think that must be when I really look totally weird and crazy to anybody I'm with. John, my most recent boyfriend, tried to understand it, but he ended up feeling hurt — I kept mixing him up with these crazy images of my dad. And eventually he left. I don't do it on purpose — I can't control it — it just happens.

Personality Splits and Spacing Out

When growing up, as soon as I heard my bedroom door open at night, I would go away, leave my body. I just didn't want to be there, didn't want to know what was being done to me, or to have to feel any of it. As an adult, when I'm feeling particularly afraid or anxious, I still find myself spacing out like that, even in situations where I know it's important to pay attention. I lose minutes, sometimes even hours. And I know it has cost me at least two jobs.

Distorted Body Image

My dad always used to say how beautiful and sexy I was, what a great body I had. He said he just couldn't help himself. But I never felt pretty or believed anybody liked me. I felt ugly and repulsive — I hated my body. I think, looking back, that the ugliness of the incest got somehow transferred to my feelings about myself and my body. As if it was all my fault he found me attractive, and that if I had been ugly, everything would have been fine.

Depression

Sexually abused children often become depressed because they have no way of dealing with their painful feelings surrounding the abuse. A child endures extreme losses (loss of trust, loss of safety, loss of self-esteem) in her life as a result of childhood sexual abuse. These losses may reinforce the depression. Most adult survivors carry these childhood losses with them and struggle with repeated bouts of depression — or they may suffer from a constant state of low-grade depression. (Low-grade depression still allows one to get through the day-to-day routines, but the person experiences little joy, and life feels futile.) Depression can be a serious illness with a number of hurtful symptoms, including

- uncontrollable emotions,
- crying jags,
- an inability to concentrate,
- anxiety,
- sleep disturbances,

- extreme change in eating resulting in significant weight loss or weight gain, and
- suicidal thoughts.

If depression is an ongoing problem for you, you should consult a doctor or psychologist, possibly both, for help. There are several ways to deal with recurring depression; one is with medication. Prescribed and monitored by a knowledgeable physician, proper medication sometimes helps to end the siege and break the cycle of a heavy bout of depression. But perhaps more important is to begin talking about and dealing with the abuse and your repressed memories of it with a professional therapist. Many adult survivors free themselves from serious depression by getting the proper help. If you find yourself feeling suicidal, don't ignore your feelings. Seek professional help immediately. Suicide or crisis hot lines can be very helpful.

When you start talking to people whom you trust about your feelings, your past abuse, the tears you have shed, and your hopes for a better future, you are on your way to making that future a reality. Go at your own pace. Talk only with people you feel safe around, and tell them only as much as you are comfortable with. Next, it's helpful to explore your personal history by talking about your childhood family. This works especially well in therapy. It will help you put your inner feelings into words and be better able to understand your feelings and yourself.

If you identify with the effects of childhood sexual abuse described in this chapter, it may be helpful for you to explore further. Knowing if and how you were abused may be an important step in the process of reclaiming your life.

CHAPTER TWO

WERE YOU ABUSED?

You were an abused child if

- you felt unloved and "unlovable" and were afraid all the time.
- you or other family members were verbally put down on a regular basis.
- you were physically hit.
- you had distant, emotionally absent parents.
- you were sexually violated.

As mentioned in Chapter One, much abuse is covert; it is not as obvious as that of physically violent parents. The crucial point is not what kind of or how often abuse occurred, but what effect it has had on the survivors and their lives. So it is important that you do not compare yourself to the people in this book and say, "Mine was not that bad."

OVERCOMING MINIMIZING THE ABUSE — A METHOD OF LOOKING INTO YOUR PAST

When they first become aware of the sexual abuse in their childhoods, most women minimize what happened to them.

Minimizing the abuse is a way they learned to cope with it when they were young. Now, the abuse may seem distant to the adult survivors. In extreme cases, they may even see it as normal.

Survivors look back at their childhoods through adult eyes. Most of them don't permit themselves to think of their child selves as vulnerable little children who were cruelly victimized. Many of them say, "It's too scary to feel that powerless and see my parents as imperfect and sometimes cruel."

A method to help you face the possibility of sexual abuse in your past is to imagine your childhood happening now to a young person you know and care about, perhaps your own son or daughter, or a niece or nephew. Does what happened to you in the past seem so trivial now? If it does, then perhaps you weren't abused. But if you feel pain in imagining another child living your experiences, then you may benefit greatly from further exploring your past with a therapist.

A young woman described childhood memories of being "slapped around occasionally," and of how her dad "looked at me funny and gave me long hugs where he would accidentally touch my breasts and comment on how I was growing up. It's really nothing very concrete," she said, "and maybe it's silly that I've let it bother me at all." I asked if she would allow her young daughter to experience such behavior from anyone. She said, "Absolutely not, she's just a little girl, and that would be wrong to do to anyone." At that point, she realized that she didn't think of herself as ever having been a little girl. Try this method of looking into your past; it can be quite helpful in determining whether you were abused.

TRISHA'S STORY:
A STORY OF MANY WOMEN

What do adults who were sexually abused as children feel like? I will describe a woman named Trisha, a composite of many women. Certainly not every adult survivor exhibits *all* these traits.

18

Trisha is thirty years old. As a child, she had been sexually molested by her uncle for years and felt she had no one to tell about it. She is having distressing memories and flashbacks when she and her boyfriend are sexual. Trisha gets depressed and has had few close relationships, so her boyfriend is very important to her, and she is afraid of losing him. She has a hard time trusting people, even when they seem to be worthy of trust. She feels distant from her alcoholic parents and then feels bad for her feelings.

Trisha is disturbed by her lack of energy and direction. Decision-making is a terrifying process for her, so she often avoids making decisions and lets things happen by default. This is further complicated by the fact that she doesn't trust her own judgments and perceptions.

She has constant anxieties and is unable to identify her feelings. It is obvious that she has had practice denying and ignoring her own feelings in her alcoholic home. Yet she is very conscious of how others might be feeling and what she needs to do to please them.

Trisha describes herself as driven — she tries to do her best and yet always feels that she falls short. She is always trying to please others and wants their approval. She also is compulsive with food, shopping, and masturbation — especially when she is anxious. When asked to describe herself, Trisha uses these words: hard worker, caring, anxious, worrier, misfit, different, angry, unusual, fearful, emotional, and overly sensitive. She did not use words such as content, peaceful, playful, humorous, intelligent, or creative.

She describes her childhood as lonely and says she felt shy and scared. She felt that she was supposed to be a perfect child and please everybody all the time. She remembers being ill a lot, wetting the bed well into grade school, having regular nightmares, grinding her teeth in bed, rocking and banging her head, and pulling and twisting out her hair. These are all indications of high stress during her childhood.

One reason Trisha sought help is because she is afraid to have children. She fears that she, or someone else, would sexually abuse them, just as she had been abused. Another reason Trisha wants help is because she feels so depressed and hopeless that she is worried she might hurt herself. She is afraid she simply can't go on if something significant doesn't change in her life. A third reason is her fear that her boyfriend will leave if she doesn't get her "sexual problem" worked out.

If Trisha had done nothing to resolve the abuse in her past, she would have continued trying to get her needs met by taking care of and trying to please other people. Because of her past, Trisha could only see two different ways to approach relationships:

1. To attach quickly and intensely with others to try to get her undernurtured childhood needs met.
2. To stay very distant from others because her childhood experience proved to her that she couldn't trust or expect anything of people.

Oftentimes these two methods of behavior become intertwined, with the resulting ping-pong effect of "don't leave me" and "get out of my life" repeated within every relationship.

Trisha wanted to be loved, yet she didn't really trust that love existed or believe she deserved it. Her behavior was very much influenced at almost every turn by the abuses and traumas of her childhood. But she began to understand this and to see how connected all her issues are. She now feels that her memories and feelings about her past can be validated. She wants to recover from the abuse, to be a healthy survivor, to be in charge of her life. Let's take a look at how this process of recovery from childhood sexual abuse begins.

BREAKING THE SILENCE

Recovering and healing from the many hurts and psychological scars of childhood sexual abuse *can* be a lengthy process, but the fact that you're reading this book means you're interested in learning about the abuse. It also indicates that you are breaking the cardinal rule learned in families who deny the abuse happened: you are choosing to break the silence. Recovery begins when you admit to yourself that something happened to you as a child. Perhaps a therapist worked with you to help you reach this point, or perhaps you did it by yourself.

Reaching Out

Once you have broken the silence, you need to reach out to other people to help you in your struggle. Just as it is nearly impossible for a practicing alcoholic to quit drinking alone, it is also difficult for an adult survivor of childhood sexual abuse to work through the emotional aftermath of the abuse without others' help and support.

There are many ways to find this help:

- therapists skilled in dealing with the problems of sexual abuse,*
- self-help groups composed of people with similar backgrounds of abuse,
- trusted friends,
- understanding clergy, and
- perhaps even other family members you trust.

Once you start talking about the abuse, it's important to explore at length your family of origin — its patterns and rules. This means not to look at how "bad" your family was, but to discover the origins of any hurtful emotional baggage you've been dragging around. You need to uncover all the things that have kept you from liking yourself and your life. At this point, it's important to begin learning techniques and attitudes that will help you feel in charge of your life.

---

* Author's note: I will suggest ways — in Chapter Twelve — to find professional help.

You Are in Charge

. Most adult survivors have strong feelings of fear, anger, hurt, and sorrow stemming from their childhood abuse. And many survivors are terrified of these feelings, of letting themselves experience them firsthand. This is probably a result of their childhood training in perfecting the art of denial. They are so adept at "tuning out and turning off" that tuning in becomes frightening. This is especially true of feelings related to their abuse. Their thinking runs along these lines: *Once I turn the feelings back on, I will be at their mercy. I don't want to relive all that pain and hurt and fear over and over again.* If you share some of these feelings, don't despair. Your feelings are normal and you can work with them a step at a time. In addition, you can get help dealing with them from professionals and other survivors.

When women in a support group for abuse survivors talk about having sad, painful feelings that haunt them day and night — feelings they can't let go of or ignore — I know they are really having difficulty being in charge of their lives and emotions and getting time-outs from overwhelming feelings. And that is why, in addition to support and phone contact between group members, they need to learn techniques that will help them take charge of their feelings.

Two very helpful techniques to handle disturbing feelings are

- letting go, and
- recognizing that you are an adult, not a child anymore — which can help you deal with your fears and emotions in a positive, action-oriented way.

Letting Go

When your emotions are about something extremely painful or traumatic, "letting go" of them may be difficult, but it isn't impossible. Take, as an example, the thoughts and emotions surrounding the impending death of a loved one. The process of dying can go on for a long and troubling time, yet your life goes on despite the emotional pain. You still need to take care of the everyday tasks of life, such as going to work, preparing your meals, taking care of children or pets, and generally getting on with the business of living.

This isn't to say you deny the sad, painful, and angry feelings about the impending death, or pretend you don't care, but instead you acknowledge that life *does* go on. You can have the painful emotions but still give yourself some breaks, some time-outs. For example, you can talk with others about your feelings, spend time with a friend, go to a movie, read a book, or take a walk in your favorite park. You wisely do whatever recharges your psychic batteries, brings feelings of happiness into your life, and gives you the strength to go on. Otherwise, letting the painful emotions dominate every waking hour would prove too exhausting, too overwhelming.

Another useful technique for letting go of painful and overwhelming emotions is to write about them in a daily personal journal. Keep track of what frightens you, of what makes you happy, sad, or mad. Whatever emotions you feel, sit down at night, open your journal, and write them down even if it is only a few sentences or key words. If you're like many survivors, you have spent years ignoring your feelings — yet you feel intensely. And remember, it's okay to feel *any* emotion without judging it. At this point, all our feelings, positive or negative, are useful information to us. Journaling is a way to have a heart-to-heart talk with yourself without feeling foolish or worrying what others may think. It's a chance to more fully know *yourself,* to be totally honest about your feelings and emotions. It's a wonderful sort of freedom.

Some women use their journals as a dumping ground for unwanted feelings. They write down what is bothering them, close the journal, put it away in a drawer — maybe lock it up — and envision all the troubles they have put down on paper as safely out of their lives for the moment. At a later time they may take the journal out and choose to think about a certain issue, but they set limits. They only do it for a limited time and then they put it out of their lives for a while. This may sound silly and contrived, but keeping a journal can be a valuable tool to help you understand and take charge of your feelings.

Recognizing Your Adulthood

You may be thinking, *I know I'm an adult now, but let's talk about something that will help me.* I can't think of a more helpful thought for an adult survivor of childhood sexual abuse to repeat to herself through the day than *I'm an adult now; I'm not a little girl that can be hurt the way I was then.* It's a key thought in recovering — to sort out memories of then from what is happening *now.*

When you recall the abuse years — whether through conscious thought, bad dreams, or involuntary flashbacks — you may feel a great deal of fear, anxiety, helplessness, or grief. That is natural. But it is crucial to remember, when experiencing those feelings, that they are *memories* of your childhood feelings. You are *not* reliving the situations themselves. You're an adult now and you have power over your thoughts and can tell them to stop. If new memories or flashbacks are overwhelming at times, then do one or more of the "letting go" techniques already discussed. Write in your journal, call a friend, attend a group meeting. If bad memories constantly intrude on your thoughts, it is important to consult a professional therapist. The therapist can offer extra guidance and possible medical aid to get you through the rough period.

You have the adult power to look at your options in any situation and choose what is best for you. A frightened child living in a nightmare world of abuse didn't have that power. Now it's time for you to take back your power. And you are doing that with each step you take: seeing a therapist, reading a book about abuse, writing in your journal, and rewriting the old rules and values that keep you trapped. Each step brings a small victory.

CHAPTER THREE

THE FAMILY OF YOUR CHILDHOOD

Looking at different types of families can help you to see your own family patterns. This will in turn help you to stop feeling responsible for the abuse you suffered or for any other of your family's ills. Other types of abuse are outlined here because many inconsistent and undernurturing families have more than one form of abuse happening within them. Here are some definitions regarding family types and other important concepts.

NURTURING FAMILY

This is a family where members pay positive and loving attention to one another's emotional and physical needs, so that they thrive as opposed to merely surviving. There is open communication and members feel free to express feelings and express privacy.

UNDERNURTURING FAMILY

This is a family that is unable to protect and provide for the psychological and physical well-being of its members at other than the most basic levels, such as food and shelter. In these families, the parents don't fulfill one or more of their roles as parents, protectors, caregivers, wage earners, and sexual partners. In such families, the parents, who themselves probably never learned appropriate ways to get their emotional needs met, turn to their children for their nurturing or sexual needs.

Making the child assume the adult responsibilities of nurturing and sex disregards the child's needs and disrespects her personal rights and the privacy of her body. At the same time, the child's emotional needs get ignored. Hence, children in these families are under-nurtured, under-protected, under-respected, and usually feel worthless and unlovable. Notice that I don't say they are *un*loved or *un*nurtured. Most children in these circumstances receive at least some nurturing. In some extremely unnurturing families, however, children receive virtually no love or nurturing. They may receive some caring from outside the family, but it is a matter of luck.

For the most part, families who are deficient or very uneven in nurturing children are, in effect, abusive families because the children don't get consistent care. In addition to sexual abuse, many of these families have overlapping forms of mistreatment, including:

- *Physical Abuse* — This includes hitting, shoving, kicking, or unusual and severe punishment (for example, being forced to stand in the corner for long and painful periods of time, or being burned with cigarettes).
- *Physical Neglect* — Some families don't provide adequate food, clothing, or appropriate shelter for family members.

- *Emotional Neglect* — This happens when family members withhold emotional care from one another and especially from the children. Consistently ignoring children's cries, their needs for verbal and physical affection, and treating them as if they are "invisible" is neglect.
- *Alcoholic Parent(s)* — Practicing alcoholic parents are emotionally absent from their spouses and children. They may also be physically and sexually abusive and neglectful of family members' needs. At best, alcoholic parents are erratic and inconsistent in their behavior, leaving children feeling unsafe, responsible, and bad.
- *Verbal Abuse* — This can be very subtle but also as blunt as a sledgehammer. When a child is ridiculed, called names, made to feel unworthy and "defective" by shaming, there may be long-term hurtful effects similar to those of violent physical abuse. Extreme efforts to control every aspect of a child's behavior violates her rights and also is abusive.

CHARACTERISTICS OF
UNDERNURTURING FAMILIES

There are some similarities between all undernurturing families. These include violations of family members' rights. There is a lack of support and neglect of nurturing within the family. Some of the most common similarities are described in the following.

Children Have Few or No Rights

Children are usually seen as extensions or property of the parents. They must look and act a certain way to gain approval. Children's boundaries may be violated through all the types of abuse, such as lack of privacy, no freedom of expression, and name-calling.

Boundaries Are Not Respected

Boundaries are the physical and psychological space that a person creates around him- or herself to be a separate and unique person from others in the world. Your boundaries define how you relate to other people and how you are willing to let them treat you.

Many people from undernurturing families have ill-defined or unprotected boundaries. For the most part, they were not encouraged to have boundaries as children, and those that they had were continually invaded by various combinations of verbal, physical, sexual, and psychological abuse. Adults who grew up in these families, looking for safety, often fall into two groups:

1. Those who seek out people who control them or whom they can control.
2. Those who are afraid of "closeness" and avoid it for fear they will get "swallowed up" by the other person.

Following are four types of boundaries that adult survivors may have learned in undernurturing families.

1. Enmeshed Boundaries

In an enmeshed relationship, the boundaries are blurred; you can't tell where one person begins and the other person ends. There is too much *we* and not enough *I* in this style of interaction.

2. No Boundaries

When you have no rules about how you want to be treated, every criticism or comment made about you comes in and is accepted as gospel truth. There is not a *me* in this system. Abusive relationships are a common result, and skillful abusers can sense when a person has no boundaries and will single her out for abuse.

3. Rigid Boundaries

Rigid boundaries keep everything — and everybody — outside. They create a sense of personal paranoia and isolation where every glance and comment can be taken as a direct affront. There is only room in this system for a *me*, and *you* can't be trusted and will be kept out.

4. Disengaged Boundaries

In this system, the disengaged person stays so far away from even the possibility of any sort of interpersonal contact or relationship that boundaries are hardly even an issue. The *I* is totally dominant and does not believe that any *we* is really necessary or possible. In this system, a person develops the same isolation as in Rigid Boundaries.

A Model of Healthy Boundaries

Ideally, your boundaries should contain and maintain your individual integrity, the *I* component. But healthy boundaries will allow you to choose to get close to people in ways that are respectful and fulfilling, thus forming *we* relationships without fear of losing or compromising your essential self.

Look at Your Boundaries

Look at the ways in which your boundaries may have been invaded or damaged by how your entire family interacted, how you specifically were treated. Draw a picture of what you think your boundaries look like. Once you're conscious of the fact that your boundaries have been damaged, you may begin healing and rebuilding them. You may have unconsciously set up defense mechanisms to protect yourself because your boundaries were not intact. Many women from undernurturing families avoid closeness, at any cost, as a way to prevent themselves from being hurt.

Parents Don't Know How to Get Their Needs Met

Parents may try to get their needs met from their mates, but usually in very indirect ways. These adults are poor at identifying needs or asking their partners for anything, most likely because they also came from undernurturing families. The parents didn't learn about getting their needs fulfilled — it wasn't modeled for them by *their* parents. They usually are uncomfortable and inexperienced in expressing their feelings. Consequently, as spouses they may develop a poor system for caring for one another and getting care back in return. This kind of interaction rarely works, and they end up turning to others to get their needs met. "Others" are frequently children, who are less intimidating than other adults.

Family Members Often Feel Hurt, Angry, or Rejected

Because some people can't communicate well about what they want, there is no mutual system of support and help. Family members often feel hurt, disappointed, and angry and rejected because it seems to them that no one cares about their wants or needs.

Parents May Be Absent

Many times one of the parents is a domineering, angry person, for example, an alcoholic father — while the mother is passive and busy trying to do everything right to please her spouse. Therefore, both may end up being emotionally unavailable to their children. The passive parent may go to the children for emotional support. So the children not only miss out on the emotional support they need, but they end up having to care for their parents.

Role Reversals

The parents may look to their children to get their needs met. A child may become a helper, confidante, or sexual partner. Many times the older children, because they are already treated as adults, do more nurturing than the parents toward the younger children.

The Family Is Isolated

Because they have difficulty sharing their feelings, parents don't have close friends outside the family. Many abusive and undernurturing families look good to those in their community. They may even be quite active within that community, but their home life is a secret and they usually remain isolated from others. This isolation increases the tendency to treat children as adults. Consequently, adult survivors often feel very guilty if they stop being their mom or dad's confidant and best friend.

There Is Never Enough

Siblings are often competitive with one another for their parents' affections. They seem to feel that if one of them is getting attention, there won't be any left for the rest of them. The undernurtured needs of these children make them easy prey to abusers, both inside and outside the family.

Children Don't Get to Be Children

The children in these undernurturing families seldom feel safe to just be kids and play. They usually carry around too many untended feelings, or they're worried about Mom and Dad — and protecting themselves and other siblings from abuse.

It's Not Okay to Talk

Abuse is a secret. Everyone may be hurt, sad, or scared of another family member, but no one talks about it. This "secret" protects the abuser and allows the family to continue operating in the accustomed way.

PERPETRATORS OF SEXUAL ABUSE

The undernurturing that can happen in families where abuse is present — with its lack of adequate love and guidance — can hurt the victimized children as much or more than the sexual abuse itself. Because abuse is a secret and because the secret is so strong and can be passed on from generation to generation, the patterns and systems it sets up are also strong. Many times sexual abuse may start from a parent to an older child. Then the abusive parent may progressively abuse the younger children. Or an abused older child may in turn abuse a younger sibling. Continuing the pattern, the younger sibling may abuse still younger brothers or sisters, or another young child in the neighborhood.

Many times there are additional problems in families where sexual abuse happens, including alcoholism or other drug abuse, physical abuse that is not sexual, verbal and psychological abuse, and chronic mental or physical illness. Any one of these factors can contribute to inconsistent nurturing of children.

The sexual abuse and the undernurturing of the children combine to negatively affect their development and learning — that is, they do not learn to feel good about themselves, to trust others or themselves. Children, however, are creative and will thus do what they can to cope.

People who sexually abuse children are usually no strangers to their victims. The abusers are mostly male and typically are close family members such as fathers, stepfathers, grandfathers, or brothers. Less often, they are mothers and sisters. Sometimes they are extended family members, friends of the family, or trusted authority figures.

The abusers may have grown up in an undernurtured family system themselves and never learned appropriate ways to get their needs met. They may turn to abusing children for a number of reasons: sexual gratification, a need for closeness, feelings of aggression, or a search for power and control.

Father or Stepfather as Abuser

The father or stepfather abuser is typically an emotionally immature man, with low self-esteem, who has little patience and is easily angered and upset. Inside he feels very powerless about his life. He translates his powerlessness into the belief that if he manipulates and controls others he will be in charge and become powerful. He probably sees himself as a victim instead of a victimizer. He may feel he has not had breaks in life and has worked hard. He might be a childhood victim of abuse himself and feels he is not appreciated for the work and money he has put into his family. He probably sees women and children as objects. The chances are good that he is also chemically dependent and has an angry, compulsive, and impulsive nature.

Abuse by her father has heavy implications for a daughter. He is her first role model of what men are like and what kind of treatment she can expect from men in positions of power and trust. Childhood sexual abuse can harm all her future male relationships and may turn her away from them.

Mothers as Perpetrators of Sexual Abuse
And as Partners of Sexual Abusers

Mothers, or women in general, are much less likely than men to sexually abuse children, but some do. The sexual abuse by mothers falls into two categories: it is either very covert or extremely cruel. The covert abuse is often verbal or under the guise of hygiene or protection, such as excessive enemas or roughly scrubbing a child's genitals to the point of pain, and even checking an adolescent's underpants to make sure he or she is not being sexual.

Some mothers who are sexually abusive to children are blatantly cruel. Such abuse is often torturous, such as burning the children's genitals with cigarettes, holding them under water until they choke, and locking them in dark closets for long periods of time and then punishing them for urinating on the floor.

Women who are partners of sexual abusers are usually passive and unassertive. They may sometimes be away from the home because of late work hours. If at home, they may be preoccupied by chronic illness or be overly involved with household chores, in addition to being emotionally absent. They may feel isolated, needy, and have a strong fear of abandonment. This reinforces their need to protect their spouses, and thus it is unlikely that they will risk confronting them. They may be physically battered by spouses and fear for their physical well-being. They may also have been sexually abused as children. Their neediness can cause them to feel overwhelmed and resentful of their children's needs.

Women abused by their mothers will struggle more in developing relationships with women. They may also feel hateful of their femaleness. Until they can clearly see the abuse as a comment on Mom and not on themselves or all women, they will stay distant and suspicious of other women.

Brothers as Abusers

Incest is a breakdown of the family system, and it is important to see sibling abuse as part of that breakdown. Brothers as abusers generally fall into two categories.

1. *Abused Abusers*

In this group, the brothers are victims of sexual abuse — or other abuse, such as beatings or neglect — from someone either inside or outside the family. They can turn sexually toward a sibling — one or more sisters or brothers to get their needs met — often copying the abuse they were subjected to.

2. *Father as Model*

In this group of brothers, sexual abuse or other aggressive and disrespectful patterns of behavior toward women are already present, with the father being the perpetrator — either overtly or covertly. Since the son learns his behavior from the father, his abuse of a sibling may be condoned and encouraged on a covert level — perhaps even overtly in extremely unnurturing families. Some females abused by their fathers have also been abused by a brother.

Being abused by a brother can be detrimental to a female's later relationships with men. For example, the ability to trust or have loving relationships may be seriously damaged. And unless as adults the abuser and victim can work through the problems and anger surrounding the abuse, maintaining a close sibling relationship is improbable.

Sisters as Perpetrators

Sisters who initiate being sexual with a younger sibling — male or female — usually fall into the "abused abuser" category. These children were sexually abused themselves and are in turn being sexual by imitating what they experienced. Sometimes they're acting out their anger and powerlessness at having been abused. Being abused by a sister shakes up a survivor's sense of trust, so she has difficulty having close, trusting relationships with other women.

Grandfathers, Uncles, and Adult Brothers-In-Law

These abusers follow typical family abuse patterns, including disrespect of women and children, and tend to exert control over others through anger. In many cases, the same grandfather or uncle who abuses a child also abused the child's mother when the mother was young. But a child victim is rarely warned about the abuser. Instead, she usually learns of her mother's childhood abuse only after telling her mother about her own abuse. This illustrates the emotional distance between the parents and the child — also the mother's denial of her own abuse. Because of that distance and lack of nurturing, the child may be more vulnerable to sexual attention from a grandfather, uncle, or other male relative.

Children sometimes say it felt special to receive so much attention from grandfather while they got little attention at home. Even though they didn't like it when he played "the game," they still sought and enjoyed the attention that went with it. But a certain helplessness also resulted from their acceptance of the abuse. They felt there was no one to talk to — that their parents wouldn't care and wouldn't stop it. Feeling special as a result of the attention associated with sexual abuse further confused their mixed-up feelings regarding sexuality and feeling loved — this is the case for many survivors.

Abusers Outside the Family

These abusers — neighbors, day-care providers, family friends, or authority figures — also show the common family patterns that go along with abuse that I've described. The common thread running through the lives of children sexually abused over a period of time seems to be that they all needed more care and attention than they got at home. In other words, they generally got little emotional support and love from their parents.

Survivors of all kinds of abuse speak of being afraid to tell their parents what happened. They also felt they had no right to do anything about the abuse. Many felt distanced themselves from their parents. Some women say they didn't tell their mothers because they felt they had to protect Mom or feared it would cause "trouble" for their family.

EFFECTS OF ABUSE

Erik Erikson developed a chart of "the ego qualities which emerge from critical periods of development."[*] The chart lays out what a child learns — tasks — at different developmental stages. The stages are consecutive and chronological. Each stage lays the groundwork for the following stage. Abuse of any sort affects these stages considerably.

What follows (next page) is a simplified version of Erikson's stages of human development. It illustrates the tasks that get completed and how they are developed. For the child to complete the tasks, parents need to

- give lots of nurturing and love.
- set realistic limits.
- leave plenty of room for individual growth as well as exploration.

The tasks the child needs to complete are the basic building blocks in order to lead the healthy, "normal" life that we have been talking about. They are necessary so the child can become a complete and contented adult. These tasks include trust, independence and self-motivation, self-identity, sense of competence, and the ability for the child to develop relationships with others and to be comfortable with herself.

---

[*] Erik Erikson, *Identity: Youth and Crisis* (New York: W.W. Norton and Co., 1968), 94.

STAGES OF DEVELOPMENT

STAGE	TASK TO COMPLETE	HOW DEVELOPED
birth to age 1 Trust vs. mistrust	Learning to give and to get	Receiving lots of nurturing, care, and admiration
age 2 Autonomy vs. shame	Acquiring independence, combating doubt and shame, learning self- control without loss of self-esteem	Continuing to be nurtured and to have reasonable limits set in a respectful way
age 3 to 5 Initiative vs. guilt	Acquiring self-motivation, overcoming guilt, developing capacity to become self-parent, acquiring self-identity	Overcoming guilt by playing, having room for develop- ment and exploration, but loving limits are set
6 years to *puberty* Mastery vs. inferiority	Achieving a sense of competence	Learning to bond with peers, learning to compete with peers, while trusting parents are there if needed
adolescent years Identity vs. nonidentity	Working on identity — to be one's self or not to be	Trying on new rules; breaking gradually away from parents, preferably with their blessing; looking at some sexual fulfillment
late adolescent, *young adult* Intimacy vs. isolation	Learning to develop a balance between being alone and with other people, being comfortable with oneself	Spending time with peers, and spending time alone

In healthy families, children are consistently nurtured and feel loved; they are competent at work and play; and they go through the stages of childhood development, gaining mastery and reinforcement as they progress. By the time they are adults in age, they are also adults mentally and emotionally. Their child selves have integrated fully into their adult selves along the way.

In an undernurturing family, the natural stages of childhood development and emotional growth are interrupted by the abuse and chronic undernurturing. It's almost always helpful for adult survivors to look at *when* the abuse happened, at what stage of development the abuse stalled them. Then they can more consciously work on the stages of development they need to master in order to be more complete and emotionally integrated adults.

Altered Coping Skills

Instead of developing the feelings about oneself and others that a child would learn in a nurturing family *(I am important; I can trust other people that I choose)*, children from abusive backgrounds will creatively alter and develop skills to survive or cope better in their undernurturing family. For example, their coping skills may include denial *(It's too painful to acknowledge, so I'll pretend it didn't happen)*, isolation *(I'm bad, and if I hide myself other people won't find that out)*, and trying to be invisible. Many of these coping skills won't work as children move out of their family into the larger community. For example, if they continue trying to be invisible they won't make friends or learn to fit in and trust people.

Each of Erikson's stages of development can result in the development of altered coping skills if the learning stage is interrupted by childhood sexual abuse, and the altered coping skills will prove ineffective in adulthood. Looking at these stages can help point out how invasive the effects of childhood sexual abuse are. For example, instead of learning trust, which brings hope, you may have learned not to trust, which brings hopelessness, depression, and isolation. Instead of learning to love and care for yourself, you may have learned to feel shame and doubt about your inner worth, which can lead to addictions and to relationships where you are further victimized. The inability to trust, feelings of hopelessness, and feelings of shame and guilt are typical of the strong psychological, emotional, and spiritual violations resulting from childhood sexual abuse. Healing brings you back to trust, autonomy, hope, closeness, and belonging.

CHAPTER FOUR

BREAKING THE SECRET, REMEMBERING THE PAST

BREAKING THE SECRET

Breaking the secret — telling another person about your sexual abuse — begins the end of your isolation. It's natural to feel anxiety at telling others of your childhood abuse. You've spent years believing you had to protect that secret. If the abuse was incestuous, you may, by breaking the secret, feel disloyal to your family and feel exposed. But you have a right to share your secret with others and thereby lessen your pain. Keeping secrets and denying the abuse put you in danger of more abuse. Speaking out breaks the cycle.

Keeping a secret, even for days or weeks, takes a lot of energy and conscious effort. Keeping a secret for years, first as a child, and then as an adult, consumes amazing amounts of energy. As one middle-aged survivor put it:

I spent so much of my young life feeling dirty and disgusting that I became extremely watchful of everything so I wouldn't be exposed as this vile little girl who, for years, had let Uncle Bob have sex with her. I spent my childhood and especially my adolescence

43

*— when the abuse was still going on — hiding
everything about myself. My whole life was one big
secret! I cry when I think of myself as that young girl
and the daily terror of being exposed as a whore,
when all the time it wasn't any of my doing at all.
No wonder I used to fantasize about laying dead in
a coffin and having my family crying because I was
gone. Then I would finally get the attention I wanted.*

Secrecy protected your abuser, allowed the abuse to continue, and controlled you as the victim. Children keep abuse secret because they're afraid of more abuse, because they're afraid no one will believe them if they do tell, and because they feel so shameful and responsible for the abuse. Breaking the secret of abuse destroys the power the abuser has over you. It is a giant step toward reclaiming your own power and letting go of the hopelessness and powerlessness of victimization.

There are many ways to break the secret, ranging from telling your therapist, friends, or your family, to actually confronting the abuser. The important thing is to first tell people you trust, so you get the support you need and deserve at such an emotionally vulnerable time. Many survivors, when they first fully understood their abuse, rushed off to tell their families and received the disbelief and total lack of support they feared so much as children. Thus, it's usually best not to tell your family until later in your recovery process.

When you break your silence for the first time, you need to tell someone who feels safe to you. The safest person is someone who won't judge you and who will listen to your story, however you decide to tell it. An old and trusted friend, a therapist, or a counselor at a women's center might all be good choices. You need to tell someone you think will be willing to accept everything at face value, without making judgments. Telling about your abuse for the first time will be the hardest. It gets easier after that first major break with the past. In general, it's a good idea to avoid discussing your abuse with co-workers or other people in situations that might later become uncomfortable for you. Think about it long and hard before you disclose information about your abuse. It's important that you talk about it, but it's also important to very carefully choose the people you talk with.

REMEMBERING

You may realize you were abused, but have only vague images or fragmented memories of the abuse. You may be frightened, wondering exactly what sort of abuse took place. That is why it may be helpful for you to be in a survivors' group with others who are trying to put the pieces of past abuse together. You need to feel safe in order to remember what happened. The more secure you feel, the easier it will be to face the facts of your past abuse. But during the remembering process, you may sometimes experience physical reactions — sometimes described as *body memories* — such as leg twitches, shaking, stomach problems, and various physical pains. Such reactions are common. You may have visual memories or emotional replays. Try to relax and let the information come. Learning to deal with your abuse, painful as it may be, will bring you relief.

It's common for abuse victims in the first stage of remembering their abuse to doubt that it happened at all. Some become convinced that — for some reason — they are only "imagining" that they were abused. Traumatic events such as childhood sexual abuse may be so frightening and shocking that our mind represses or "loses" the memories. This is because they are too painful to think about. You need to trust your gut feeling. If you have strong, recurrent feelings that you were abused as a child, you owe it to yourself and your peace of mind to explore these feelings. If you keep thinking something bad happened to you, it probably did. "Putting the memory pieces together reconstructs real

45

events you can deal with and dispels the terror of nightmare images and pieces of memories that make you feel crazy,'' said a veteran group member to a newcomer.

How to Remember:

- *Begin by writing down what you do know and remember.* You will build from there.
- *Write an autobiography.* Your therapist, if you are seeing one, may have a history form with questions for different stages of life. Write about how you felt as a child at each age. Write about home, yourself, school, friends, family, and any major events.
- *Look at family photos.* Use each photo as a trigger for what happened during that period of your life. What happened that day? What did it feel like to be there?
- *Go to supportive family members, friends, and neighbors to get more information.*
- *Close your eyes and try on a memory to see how it fits and if it brings anything else to mind.*
- *Write about or tell your therapist about your dreams, particularly any recurrent ones from childhood.* They may be a key to what you have repressed. Recurring dreams may be about someone coming into your room, a monster in the closet, or something trying to hurt you. Pay close attention to these dreams and try to understand what they mean. But remember, since dreams are generally not factual, the images may be symbolizing something else that our unconscious is trying to work out or master.
- *Pay attention to strong feelings you have in certain situations, and trust them.* You may be making a connection with something in your past.
- *If possible, visit the neighborhood where you lived as a child.* What kinds of memories come back to you?

- *If you're seeing a therapist, it may be helpful to work with the process of imagery regarding events in your past.* Guided imagery allows you to safely remember and revisit places and events through your mind. You now have your adult self to keep you safe. You may gain a sense of power through working on your story with a therapist.

The Child Within

Since the sexual abuse took place in your childhood, it's necessary for your recovery to focus on what you were like as a child. This is important, since our child self lives on inside each of us and exerts considerable power over our life. It will help you to reconstruct an accurate image of who you were as a little girl. For some adult survivors, that little child, or "child within," is so painfully present that they have trouble separating from her to live today. Whether you need to become reacquainted with your child within or you need to detach from her, the following steps will help you to understand how she was shaped. You need to know this to have compassion for her and nurture her — without letting her and her childhood fears control your adult life. These steps are also a beginning point for you to reparent yourself as a child and to deal with the intense feelings surrounding your abuse.

- *If possible, examine photos taken before and after the abuse took place.* Can you see differences? Talk about them with your therapist, group members, or people you trust. Talk about what you think the girl in the pictures is feeling and thinking.
- *Write a letter to the child in the picture.* Get a correspondence going with her. Get out paper and crayons, and let her respond to your correspondence with scribbles, pictures, or words. It can be a very powerful exchange, giving both of you new strength and information.

- *Write out specific incidents of the abuse and share them with your group or therapist.* This will help take away the power and fear the incidents have held over you.
- *Rewrite scenarios from your childhood to reflect how you would have liked your ideal childhood to be.* This will help you regain some of the things you didn't get and will help you grieve losses and give you more ideas for what you want your life to be.
- *Learn new ways to play, to feel good about yourself.* Try spending some time around children and imagine your inner child being with them and playing with them. How would you have felt as a child playing with them? What would you now do for yourself to feel better?
- *In using guided imagery with your therapist, or alone, spend some time nurturing your inner child and playing with her.* Tell her you know things are tough, but they'll get better and she is a good person whom bad things have happened to. Reassure her that none of it was her fault.

GRIEVING YOUR LOSSES

Taking care of unmet needs from your childhood will help you move on with your life. As you remember what your childhood was really like, you may become more aware of all the losses you suffered. At some point, it will be helpful for you to identify and grieve for the losses, for what the abuse deprived you from as a child. Grieving can mean having a range of feelings from disbelief to sadness, to anger, to even rage. You deserved to be loved, admired, protected, and playful, but past abuse can mean you didn't get or didn't learn these things in your childhood home. Here are some losses adult survivors most commonly talk about. Some of them may fit for you, while others may not. How many do you identify with?

- Loss of trust
- Loss of safety
- Loss of soft cuddly feelings
- Loss of loving parents
- Loss of friends
- Loss of the ability to play
- Loss of learning
- Loss of positive attitude toward life
- Loss of being in touch with own body
- Loss of hope
- Loss of healthy relationships
- Loss of sisters and brothers who care
- Loss of personal opinions and thoughts
- Loss of personal space and things
- Loss of self-esteem
- Loss of having parents as an adult
- Loss of grandparents for children

The Little Girl that Was

Talk about your losses with a trusted friend, your therapist, or other group members. This will allow you to learn compassion for the little girl who survived and endured all the hurts, pains, and fears you feel now as you remember your past. Let yourself cry for the little girl you were, who grew up without having some of her most basic childhood needs met. Being vulnerable and feeling sad are not weaknesses. Sharing your feelings opens you to the whole range of emotions, allowing you to connect with others. Controlling and hiding your feelings may make you feel safer, but you will also feel lonely and will be closed off to change. Expressing your grief will be a way to get over some of your intense negative feelings. Sharing with others who care will help heal your hurts and loneliness. You won't ever have to be alone with all those feelings again. One survivor wrote the following about the first time she dared break part of her secret:

The first relationship I ever felt trust in or felt really cared about for who I really was, was with my therapist. I told a little bit about my abuse, just to see how she would respond. She leaned forward, she listened, and she didn't put me down. She respected my feelings, and there was compassion in her face and voice. This was closer to real love and nurturing than anything I ever got in my family. At that moment I felt grief-stricken for myself as a little girl. I had wanted something like this, but didn't think it existed.

Or if it did, I was sure I didn't deserve it. I broke down crying. I was never more aware of just how much sadness I had until that day. It was tapped into by someone's caring.

Grief is an especially important emotion for those who were abused or had other great losses as children — such as the death of a parent. A childhood lost to sexual abuse needs to be grieved just as does a dead parent. As you look closely at your childhood family, you will probably feel grief over missing your childhood. When you become aware of your grief, you can do your grieving and feel some release. Though that may sound dreary and heavy, grieving makes room in your life so other people and new feelings can enter it. You will still feel sadness about the things you lost or never had, but it won't keep you from moving on to a better life.

REPRESSED ANGER

Anger is another important emotion, a natural defense reaction when someone or something violates us. You may call it anger, irritation, annoyance; it all stems from the feeling of violation. Anger tells you something is wrong and that you need to act. Many survivors were never allowed by their abusers or their families to express anger. Often, they turn this repressed anger back on themselves in a self-destructive manner.

You may not feel anger now, but you may feel that way as you quit feeling responsible for the abuse. Many survivors start to get angry when they become aware of all they lost in their childhoods. Expressing anger is a way to stand up for your inner child and say the abuse was *wrong*.

Many survivors of childhood sexual abuse fear anger because they frequently saw angry people lose control and become violent. Some grew up feeling anger was wrong. Maybe for you, the easiest way to feel your anger will be to first feel anger toward someone else's abuse. Does this story from a sister survivor make you feel anger toward the abuser?

> *I've always been afraid of anger. Both my parents regularly drank, cursed, and threw things. I prayed they wouldn't kill one another. I never dared complain or say much. When my babysitter's husband, Ed, began to be sexual with me at nap time, I didn't dare tell my parents. Ed, a school teacher, told me I would go to jail if anyone found out, and he gave me treats to help buy my silence. As he progressed from fondling to penetrating me with his finger, then with little objects, and on to intercourse by age nine, I knew how wrong it was and felt it was all my fault. But I felt there was no place to go and no one to tell, no one to help or protect me. I wanted to die at nine years old. I don't remember feeling any anger about the abuse until I was listening to one of the other survivors in group tell her story. I felt so sad for her as we passed around her childhood pictures. Then I was suddenly struck by an overwhelming rage at all the people who abused her and at all the others who didn't love her or protect her. She was just like me and it made me furious.*

51

Have you allowed yourself to feel anger at what happened to you? Do you feel anger toward your abuser? Expressing your anger is a way to work through it. Your anger can give you energy to get yourself going; it can help push you along the road to recovery. Your anger is your friend. As long as you use your anger appropriately and aren't mean or verbally abusive to others, it can be a positive force in your life. But, taken too far, anger can turn into violent rage and become destructive.

Rage Hurts You

Some survivors feel angry and rageful all the time. Maybe you experience this kind of all-consuming rage and anger. If you do, it probably gets in the way of having relationships and feeling good about yourself. You may waste all your energy fantasizing about revenge and punishments for your abusers. Usually this kind of rage comes from feeling betrayed by the abuser.

Survivors who feel constant anger and rage need to find some way to let go of these emotions. The rage ends up costing you much more than it could ever cost your abusers. It is also a way your abusers still have you in their control. Do some writing or talk to someone about your rageful feelings. Up to a point, your rage may have been protecting you from more hurt, but you need to get support for letting go of it so you can move on to more rewarding emotions and actions.

SHAME IS PERVASIVE

When children aren't consistently loved or nurtured, they feel unlovable and bad. This is the most hurtful part of sexual abuse, and it colors everything a survivor thinks or feels about and how she interacts with others. If you were sexually abused or undernurtured as a child, you may be left with a low self-image, including feelings of self-loathing and self-hate. Another name for these feelings is *shame*. No matter how successful, smart, nice, and attractive you look to others, chances are you describe yourself as ugly, defective, stupid, and perhaps even as evil. You may try to be perfect and look perfect, but underneath the perfectionism is a vulnerable child who feels unlovable and bad. This is what shame does to you.

Shame is so pervasive that it affects what you hear other people say to you. You may react negatively to comments that were not meant that way, and you may even "hear" things that were never really said! Here are some ways to get out and stay out of your shame:

- *Recognize shame, label it.* This takes away some of its power over your life.
- *Remember that shame is not about who you are.* It is about how you were parented and treated as a child.
- *Buy a book of affirmations to read daily and apply them to your life so you begin thinking of yourself in positive ways.*
- *As a friend, write yourself an affirming letter, emphasizing your good points.* Take out the letter and read it when you feel down or shameful.
- *Call a friend and get a boost when you feel shameful.* Let your friend know how you're feeling, and ask for some positive affirmations.

You need to make peace with your past. Ignoring and denying the abuse you suffered in your childhood will keep you from being free to live your life to the fullest. Acknowledging your abuse and talking about it with other people will help you let go of it and deal with its consequences in a healing and adult manner. You will be able to grieve your losses and to build a positive relationship with yourself today. You can heal your damaged self-image and at last lay claim to your future. A way of accomplishing this healing is described in the next chapter, "Parenting and Reparenting Yourself."

CHAPTER FIVE

PARENTING AND REPARENTING YOURSELF

The way we were treated as small children is the way we treat ourselves the rest of our life.

—*from* For Your Own Good
by Alice Miller

Learning to feel lovable — capable and worthy of being loved — is the most powerful feeling of all. It opens the door for us to connect with other people; it keeps out shame; it inspires us to re-create our life according to our dreams. As our lovableness quotient increases, so do our feelings of self-esteem. If we are not in charge of our self-esteem, someone else will be. And that is not what we want.

PARENTING AND REPARENTING

In most families where abuse happened, the lack of adequate parenting cuts victims off from feelings that non-abused children take for granted. Here are some things you need to look at and change in order to set your life right through a growth process that involves parenting and reparenting yourself.

Our Internal Parent

We all have internal voices that speak to us. Yours may say things such as: *That was stupid. . . . Why did you say that? . . . You really are lazy, aren't you?* If this sounds familiar, it probably means you internalized the verbal abuse, shame, or neglect you received as a child and are recycling it to yourself every day. As an experiment, stop yourself the next time you're aware of the critical inner voice and ask, *Now who was that talking to me just then? Was that my mother, watching over my shoulder, continuing her constant criticism of me?* I think you'll find this an interesting and instructive exercise. Once you realize the source of your negative comments, it will be easier for you to take steps to get rid of them.

Creating a Loving Parent

Think about any positive things you got from your parents. Even in the worst cases, there almost always are some positive aspects.

Don't worry if you can't think of anything good; you may not be able to see the good through your present feelings, or maybe there really was nothing. Think of all the best elements you remember your friends getting from their parents — the things you may have envied. Add to that all the caring people who have made you feel special and loved. Put these elements together in your imagination with the most loving, nurturing Mom you can think of.

It may seem silly at first to consciously think up a very loving and nurturing parent for yourself. But remember, we're creating a way for you to think of yourself as a person who deserves to be taken care of and kindly and lovingly nurtured. Too often, survivors live their lives taking care of others and providing for others' needs. They keep up a steady internal barrage of negative comments — all the old shaming messages from the past — about themselves.

A Vigilant Parent

Your newly created, internal parent can be on vigil twenty-four hours a day. When she hears those old criticisms creeping into your thoughts, she can tell that shaming voice to go away, that it isn't needed or wanted anymore. I encourage survivors to speak aloud to themselves and tape affirmations to their cupboard, so they hear their messages and see them as well as think them. It can feel very soothing, hearing this new, caring, parental voice telling you how well you did. As you practice listening to your internal, nurturing parent, you will start canceling out the abusive messages from the past.

Some survivors have counted the number of negative messages they give themselves each day and have been astounded at the constancy — forty to fifty negative messages daily aren't unusual. As long as you're going to talk to yourself, you might as well be nice. As Walt Kelly's comic strip character, Pogo Possum, so clearly put it: "We have met the enemy and he is us." Unfortunately, for most adult survivors of childhood sexual abuse, this is all too true. But you can change things for the better.

Taking Responsibility

You do have to be careful that your newly created internal parent doesn't become a sugary mom who constantly lets you off the hook from being responsible for your behavior or keeps you from taking any risks at all. You don't want your parent to be an enabling person who says, *Oh that's okay, you don't have to take that job; it is too hard.* Or, *That's too scary; don't even try it.* You need to parent yourself to make the best choices for yourself. This is part of being a fully functional adult. You take responsibility for your own life and happiness.

Parenting and reparenting let you start meeting some of your formerly ignored childhood needs — ones that have been getting in the way of having adult friendships and love relationships.

- You can now approve of yourself.
- You can have loving and respectful friends.
- You can take time out to have fun.
- You can know you are strong enough to leave an abusive relationship.

Your internal parent can be as creative as you like in constructing a safe, caring world for you to replace the scary, unpredictable one of your childhood. You can imagine yourself going back in time and nurturing your inner child in ways you have always felt were needed. You can hold her and tell her that the abuse isn't her fault. You can let her know you won't let her be abused again. In your imagination, you can even call the police and have the abuser put in jail or treatment. Talk to yourself aloud. Make your positive parenting as conscious and obvious as you can. It will help undo the negative parenting you grew up with and eventually drown out those old, unwanted voices. This parenting process is very healing and can relieve the negative emotions of loneliness, shame, and guilt.

It can be both fun and healing to go back to fun activities from the period of time your abuse took place. Coloring books are an easy and inexpensive way to start. Riding a bike, roller skating, and picnics are but a few other ideas. If you aren't ready to share your playing with peers, take an adult education class in swimming, drawing, sculpture, or music at your level.

SEPARATING THE ABUSED CHILD
FROM THE ADULT

Creating an internal nurturing parent helps separate your inner child from your adult self. Most survivors have a hard time feeling like complete adults. So much of their un-resolved childhood abuse is active in their lives that they often continue to respond like children.

Linda, a nurse, one day found herself hiding in a closet at the hospital where she worked and couldn't understand what was going on with her. She had been afraid and anxious numerous times before when patients had casts on — or when new staff members started working with her. But hiding in the closet terrified her. As she put it, "My rational mind was saying, *What are you doing? You can't leave your patients and go hide. You're an adult.*" She was sure that she was going crazy and would have to quit her job. She was getting more and more anxious and paranoid about going to work.

When she came to me to find out if she was crazy, I felt fairly sure that she was reliving some traumatic childhood event. After some time in therapy, it came out that when she was a child, her mother took her along when she went to care for a semi-invalid uncle for a few months. He had fallen and broken some bones — she remembered the casts. Her mom would leave her alone with him while she cooked meals, did the laundry in the basement, hung out the wash, and did other chores. Linda was supposed to entertain her uncle and take care of him while her mother did this work. Linda was four years old.

The uncle was sexually abusive and mean to her. He threatened her with throwing her down the stairs and break-ing her arms if she told her mother what was going on. Linda had completely repressed all of this, yet found herself replay-ing parts of the abuse in many areas of her life.

As we explored further, she realized how much these abusive events had shaped her life: her fear of men, her in-security, her becoming a nurse, her seemingly irrational fear and hatred of casts. It all began to make sense to her.

Survivors like Linda can't simply leave their past behind. It's not that easy. The past, for her, is very much in the present. She needed to learn to separate her past so it didn't affect her present. Then, when she had reactions of anxiety, she could speak to herself in a very nurturing voice, and say, *That is my inner child wanting to hide in the closet. I am an adult now, and my uncle can no longer victimize me. I have the power to take care of myself, even to refuse to care for an abusive patient.*

She can soothe her inner child and still be a competent adult. In time, the stressful and regressive episodes diminished, and she was never again so incapacitated by anxiety that she couldn't function as an adult. She began to enjoy her life and work much more fully.

For many survivors, unlike Linda, the memories of abuse are not forgotten and hidden away — in fact, the victims often wish they were. The memories of sexual abuse — the images, nightmares, and anxiety attacks — are always in their conscious mind. For others, awareness of the abuse comes by slowly remembering it, piece by piece. In some cases, it may come back in one explosive, almost overpowering flashback while watching a movie, reading a book, or hearing a story that triggers a spontaneous memory of the abusive events. For all of these women, it is important to reparent their inner child and separate her from their adult self, so they may become whole and competent.

If you have flashbacks of your abuse, you need to keep telling yourself that the abuse isn't happening again. The flashbacks are only memories, and they can't hurt you. Take the entire process as slowly as you wish, and have supportive people around to help you deal with the difficult issues and feelings that arise. In other words, you are now a competent adult and fully capable of coping with the memories, painful as they may seem.

Many survivors consider hypnotism as a way to immediately remember all the details of abuse. Generally, I haven't found this practice helpful. And it can be harmful to people who remember more than they are capable of handling, early in their recovery. Trust in the *process* of remembrance

— your painful memories will surface as you are emotionally capable of processing them. More than anything, the process of remembrance is a very individual one for each survivor.

Support groups of women healing from sexual abuse are important to the reparenting process. Some women need to talk about each remembered event as a way to let go of the past. Others don't feel the need to share many specific events of their past, but may instead talk about how small and how scared they still feel in many adult situations. Each survivor needs to share some of her past to break the strong *no talk* rule, moving at her own pace. Some may need to cry often and long; others will frequently be angry; and still others may want to work on things in a different way. There are many paths to choose from, but they all lead to a common destination: freedom from the tyranny of the past.

CHAPTER SIX

RECOGNIZING YOUR STRENGTHS

Like so many adult survivors of childhood sexual abuse, you probably feel some shame about yourself and the abuse you suffered. On some level, you probably even feel responsible that it happened. These feelings are normal because of the shame and secrecy surrounding childhood sexual abuse. Your abuser may even have implied or told you that you were responsible that it happened, but that is untrue.

Children do whatever they can to cope with and survive unpleasant or dangerous situations. That may mean "going along" with the abuse to avoid making it even worse. Many abused children and teens also don't tell anybody what is happening to them. They fear they will be blamed or that it will cause trouble and pain for people they love. These confusing and conflicting feelings are far beyond what is normal for a child to deal with. Children are supposed to feel protected and safe at home, but the abuse robs them of a good part of their childhood by taking away their innocence, and filling them with secrets, hurts, and fears.

You may be aware of times when, as a child, your fear of upcoming abusive episodes made you be "creative" in thinking of ways to avoid or minimize the physical or emotional pain. Children learn ways to cope with the fear that there is going to be "trouble" for them again. You may have become an overachiever, a "good" kid, a "tough" kid, anything to protect yourself from the painful repetition of abusive behavior. Maybe you pretended to be asleep or otherwise numbed yourself to the experience. Or you may have used alcohol and other drugs to dull the pain of verbal and psychological sexual abuse. Whatever your choice of defensive weapons, chances are your methods of coping with the abuse are still with you today. Some methods may be hurtful to you, but others may be useful as a source of strength in your recovery. What follows in this chapter is a summary of the most common coping mechanisms children use to deal with abusive episodes and to try to make their world make sense.

DISSOCIATING FROM PAINFUL SITUATIONS

Many adult survivors of childhood sexual abuse learned to dissociate or emotionally remove themselves from the reality or awareness of the abuse. This helped them diminish or avoid some of their physical and emotional pain. Some survivors had a sensation of leaving their bodies during the abuse and traveling somewhere else or being aware of the abuse only as an uninvolved observer. Others speak of going into a trance during the abuse and losing time. They may have focused all their attention on a particular thought or object, such as a night-light in their room. The effect was the same: disconnecting from what was being done to them.

Did you dissociate as a child? Is it something that you still do when you are in a situation that makes you feel nervous or fearful? The downside is that it may prevent you from connecting with other people. Or you may feel it is "crazy" behavior. But it isn't crazy. You learned it as a normal and healthy response to an abnormal and abusive situation. Carried to extremes in your adult life, however, it can be harmful. For example, at times that require your adult attention, such as a meeting at work, you may disconnect from your adult self and become the child who was abused. But, as you feel stronger about yourself, you should find that you dissociate less frequently.

In a milder and more controlled form, dissociation is a way of *letting go* or *detaching* from an event, thing, or person so you don't become obsessed or burnt out. Detachment and letting go are deliberate actions, unlike strong dissociation, and are helpful tools that some people have difficulty learning to use. It's worthwhile, however, to learn to use them correctly.

Daydreaming of Better Worlds

Many survivors talk about the elaborate worlds they created in their daydreams to avoid the harsh reality of an abusive home. For example, one woman spoke of the many hours she had spent daydreaming of a beautiful grove of trees and wildflowers. There, she had fun with imaginary parents and make-believe friends, totally blocking out her real life — that of abusive parents and loneliness. Another woman had pretended that her abusive father was not her real dad at all, but some mysterious clone who was deceiving everyone but her. In her daydreams, her real father would come and rescue her, destroying her abuser and setting her free.

Because of their need to escape an unacceptable reality, many survivors develop a stronger, more vivid imagination than most people. Their acute sense of imagery and visual detail, along with strong story-telling abilities — all sharpened by their many hours building imaginary worlds — often result in superior creative abilities, such as in writing, drawing and painting, and dance.

Caretaking of Others

Some women feel they have to fix everything, take care of the needs of others, and generally try to make everybody but themselves happy. They learned to be extremely sensitive to others' needs, hoping that this would prevent further abuse. This endless tap dance around other family members gave some sexually abused children the illusion of safety and power: if they took good care of everybody, maybe the abuse would stop. This caretaking behavior continues into adult relations as they continue trying to please others.

Are you a chronic caretaker of people? You don't have to be. As you begin to like yourself and trust others, you can let people like you without waiting on them like a slave and trying to run their lives. It's more important that you learn to live your own life, for yourself. Then others can learn to accept you on your own terms and for who you really are. You can then use the tremendous energy you expend on others in healthier ways: you can do things for yourself and those you care about because you *want to*, instead of feeling that you *have to*. It's fun to do things for others and care about them when it's a two-way relationship.

Repressing and Denying the Memories

Repression and denial, though not so extreme, may have the same effect as dissociation. You simply don't let yourself have feelings about what happened. You may have denied the abuse or repressed it for so long that when images and memories begin coming back after ten, twenty, thirty, or more years, they can make you feel crazy. At first, the memories may feel like waking dreams, nightmares, or hallucinations causing you to feel disoriented. And yet, you may also feel that those nightmares were, at one time in the past, your real experience; this awareness can be terrifying.

Along with repression and denial, many adult survivors experience distortion of reality. Their families not only denied what happened, but may have even tried to make it into something positive. One woman told this story:

When Dad got violent, Mother would pack us kids into the car and leave. She would say we were going on a big adventure. We not only didn't talk about our feelings and what was happening, but she made it into something fun! I grew up in so much denial that I feel I am desensitized to things — like my husband's meanness and verbal abuse. I also let my boss put me down in front of clients without reacting to it. It's as if, at some level, I trick myself into believing it's for my own good or that everyone acts like that — even though I know they don't.

Do you identify with these thoughts about denial, repression, and distortion of reality? If so, it's important that you talk to others about your feelings. This will help you validate those feelings and let you more objectively consider how they affect you.

Once you get over your fear of life outside your circle of repression and denial, you will find that you have a good sense of "radar" that alerts you when someone is abusive to you. And you will develop the strength necessary to either avoid it or put a stop to it. You will come to be an excellent judge of character.

Survivors are perceptive at reading other people. And they are generally empathic and caring because of what they went through. Once you understand why you developed your coping behaviors to survive the abuse you endured, you can learn to see the positive side of those coping behaviors and use them as skills in your work and in your private life.

Self-Imposed Isolation

Many adult survivors become loners, or they at least avoid intimate relationships. They may be fearful of trusting people since they were sexually violated as children by those they trusted. This self-imposed isolation keeps them from further abuse and hurt, but it also deprives them of getting their needs met. Many women decided as young children to never trust that their parents or anyone else will be there for them. This was a way for them to cut their losses at an early age — and is probably something they continue to do in adulthood.

Women who have become loners may be frightened of disclosing personal feelings to a group of people, as in therapy. Although doing so is alien to their philosophy of survival in isolation, most survivors stay in a support group to work through their anxiety. They already know how painful and empty the loneliness feels.

Loneliness, however, is different from *being alone*, and we can all benefit from understanding the distinction. We all need some time alone, to reflect on our life, to think over the events of the day, and to plan for the day ahead. These are things that help us get to know ourselves. This is not loneliness; it is choosing to be alone. True loneliness comes from cutting ourselves off from others, when we really want to be close to them. We all need time to be with people — it's part of being human. As we learn to trust and share more with people, our sense of loneliness will diminish, and our ability to choose to be alone, when that is our wish, will improve.

Converting Emotional Pain to Physical Ills

Some children from undernurturing families discover they are nurtured more if they are sick. Some of these traumatized children feel safer changing their emotional pain into physical problems, so instead of repressing bad feelings, they transfer them to parts of their bodies. Chronic stomach problems, leg shakes or twitches, self-destructive behavior, vomiting, and migraine headaches are all common to adult survivors. Some survivors turn to cutting or mutilating themselves, which is a self-destructive way of expressing repressed feelings. Others feel more powerful and in charge of their hurts. As feelings get expressed and the person no longer feels shameful, the self-mutilation stops.

If you have a history of psychosomatic (self-induced) illnesses, don't be too upset about it. In some ways, they can actually be beneficial to you. For example, physical symptoms such as an upset stomach or "nervous" headache can be very strong warnings. They could indicate that you are under too much stress or denying the impact of a job setback on your life.

Listen to your body, and listen to your physician too. Psychosomatic illnesses can mean that you need to make some important decisions. They may be an "early warning system" about painful events that are happening to you. They may even be connected with working through your history of sexual abuse. Stressful memories may be triggering physical reactions. One woman's chronic nausea was connected to the terror and loneliness of her childhood. Now she's learning to identify her feelings of fear and loneliness as soon as, and sometimes before, she gets ill.

Numbing Out and Turning Off Feelings

"Numbing out" was described this way by one adult survivor:

> It's like turning off my feelings by a switch. I can live my life this way, very removed from what is going on around me. Sometimes it's like watching a movie. If something is funny, I can laugh; if it's sad, I might cry. But it is all done vicariously, as if everything is happening to another person, not to me.

Another survivor remembered exactly the day she turned her feelings off:

69

I was not going to ever again let him see that he had hurt me. It was the only power I had. He could do anything he wanted to me physically, but not emotionally.

If you live your life numbing your feelings, you're missing out on many of the good things life has to offer. As you begin to heal, you will find it easier to let your guard down. You can allow yourself to feel any emotion without pretending it is happening to someone else. Most importantly, you will learn to use that numbing out ability to selectively detach from harmful people or situations. Detachment is a valuable skill; you just have to learn the appropriate times to use it.

Turning to Addictions and Other Compulsive Behavior

Substance abuse or a preoccupation with food, sex, or gambling as a way of coping with life may lead to addiction. Alcoholics, other drug addicts, and people who overeat or have sex compulsively all start out trying to make themselves feel better by soothing or medicating themselves with the drug or the behavior. They learn that the object of their compulsion can *seem* to make them feel whole. In fact, it can make them feel almost magically happy — at least for a while. But addictive and compulsive behaviors, such as overeating, only feel good for the moment and afterwards can result in the person feeling very shameful. Some survivors feel that while overeating made their childhoods seem bearable, the food sneaking and weight gains contributed to their feelings of badness and shame.

Others say drug abuse gave them the illusion of finally feeling good about themselves. It also allowed them to do things they had never done before — such as dating, asking for a raise, or being sexual by their own choice. But the overriding motivation behind the drug abuse was that they didn't hurt so much anymore. The thought of letting go of their addictions or compulsive behaviors can, at first, seem terrifying to adult survivors. But it is a necessary part of recovery.

Maintaining an unhealthy addiction requires an inner drive and intense energy. That same drive and energy can be used in recovery to run your life and to get your wants and needs met by healthy human interaction. As you get used to caring for yourself, you will also learn the inner peace that comes from being honest with yourself and with others. You can benefit from the overall feeling of goodness that comes from being physically active and eating a healthy, well-balanced diet. Once you learn to harness that compulsive energy, your possibilities are endless.

Accepting Blame for Abuse

Accepting blame is a powerful survival skill for children as a way to feel in charge of their world. All children want to see their parents as good and loving so they feel safe. It's less scary for children to feel bad than to see their mom and dad as abusive, to be unprotected, or feel uncared for. As an adult, when you are able to accept the powerlessness you felt as a child, you can turn to what you can be now: in charge of your life and your options.

It isn't the coping skills you developed in childhood that are bad for you; it's the uses to which you put them. During recovery, there are opportunities for you to turn the same coping skills into positive forces. Recovery can help you see that you really do have choices on how you feel and behave. Remember, however, that old behaviors don't change overnight; it takes time and practice to learn new ones.

CHAPTER SEVEN

ALCOHOL OR OTHER DRUG ABUSE

One or more family members in a family where there is sexual abuse is also likely to abuse chemicals. In fact, if you were sexually abused as a child, there is a more than 50 percent chance that alcohol abuse or other drug abuse was also present in your family.

Ten percent of the general population is generally considered to be alcoholic. But in families where a child is sexually abused, that percentage jumps up tremendously. Not surprisingly, many teenage and adult survivors of childhood sexual abuse also turn to alcohol or some other addiction in misguided attempts to cope and to deal with their pain.

In this chapter, we look for answers to three important questions:

1. Why do so many adult survivors of abuse become addicted to alcohol and other drugs or have other compulsive behaviors such as overeating or sexual addiction?
2. Why do families where childhood sexual abuse occurs also have such a high rate of alcohol abuse and alcoholism?

3. Why is there a greater chance that a child from a home where the parents abused chemicals will become sexually abused from either inside or outside of the family?

Although different types of drug abuse (alcohol, cocaine, marijuana, heroin) each cause particular types of behaviors, I will talk most often about alcohol abuse or alcoholism, since it is still the most common drug problem in this country. Alcoholism is more apt to develop in people with an alcoholic parent than in those whose parents were not alcoholic. Practicing alcoholics also generally have low self-esteem. This is often a result of growing up in emotionally undernurturing families where their feelings weren't adequately expressed or addressed. When children are undernurtured, they often feel shameful and defective — they feel they are unloved because something is wrong with them.

Unlike those from nurturing and stable families, people from chaotic and undernurturing families don't learn healthy and complete ways to get their needs met. This may leave them feeling incomplete, always lacking. Alcohol is often seen as a "perfect quick fix" to fill these hollow feelings. For a time, drinking or other drug use can make a person feel whole, even euphoric. But, of course, that passes and the result of continually chasing after the "quick fix" is usually addiction. Alcoholism or any other drug addiction is a disease and is responsible for an incredible amount of pain and misery in the world.

THE LIE OF ALCOHOLISM AND SEXUAL ABUSE

Children who are abused feel unsafe, unloved, and they often are told they are responsible for the abuse. If members of the family also abuse alcohol or are alcoholic, the child is subjected to even more abuse and neglect. And, in some cases, the person's drinking episodes result in physical violence. The alcohol abuse is just one more family secret that is denied, further distorting the child's view of reality.

This is the essential lie of any kind of drug addiction and of sexual abuse — that it isn't happening. The children learn to distrust their own feelings and perceptions as a result of this denial, but especially related to sexual abuse, they also learn to distrust everyone around them. They distrust the sexual abuser for violating them, and they learn they can't trust other family members and adults outside the family who do nothing to stop the abuse.

In families torn by both sexual abuse and drug abuse, victimized children find it doubly hard to come to terms with their lives, let alone try to do something about it. The feelings involved are painfully clear in this woman's story:

When I was in grade school, I'd often come down from upstairs and find my mom crying at the kitchen table. She'd tell me how awful it was, being married to my dad, and that she only stayed for us kids. I heard their horrible fights — I knew it was true. I felt so guilty about it all. There was no way I could tell her what Dad was doing to me when she worked nights. At times, I wanted so desperately for her to notice how I felt and to ask me what was wrong. But she was off in her own world of pain and I wasn't going to make it worse. Besides, I thought Dad's drinking and the abuse were my fault. I feared Mom would also blame me.

Alcoholism in Adult Survivors

Alcoholism in a family also harboring sexual abuse is one more "awful" secret. It adds to the denial of each victim's feelings and to each person's isolation from other family members and the community at large. As adult survivors struggle to cope, they may turn to alcohol or other drugs to get through everyday life and to dull their nightmares, the residue of an abused childhood.

Alcohol use is an easily adopted means to cope. Adult survivors whose parents or parent were alcoholic are prone to adopting those alcoholic behaviors they saw modeled. And alcohol and other drugs were probably readily accessible in these families. In some cases, abusers gave alcohol to their victims when abusing them.

Many women say that when they first started using alcohol or other drugs, it felt like they had finally found a way to feel good and to be in control. But, of course, they sunk even deeper into the emotional hole. And trying to deal with the dual problems of alcoholism and childhood sexual abuse can be very difficult. The good news is that many survivors have tackled both problems and now lead much happier and fulfilled lives; their struggles can help you.

Sobriety Alone Does Not Cure the Effects Of Childhood Sexual Abuse

Recovering alcoholics who were sexually abused may still feel "defective" after years of hard-won sobriety. They commonly hope that after getting sober, they won't have to talk about or deal with the abuse — that sobriety will be enough. But for many, it isn't that simple. The effects of childhood sexual abuse don't disappear with sobriety.

In fact, many women find that the longer they're sober, the more memories of the abuse float to the surface of their minds. This happens because their denial is fading, and they feel stronger and find it "safer" to remember.

This phenomenon brings many alcoholic survivors into therapy. They are afraid their intense feelings will set off their drinking again. These women may feel hopeless and despairing — and "cheated" — that sobriety hasn't solved this aspect of their past. Their feelings, if left untreated, are indeed capable of sending them back to drinking or other drug use. If you are one of these recovering women, it's especially important for you to come to terms with the sexual abuse, so it doesn't endanger your sobriety.

Some adult survivors are lucky enough to meet other recovering alcoholics with sexual abuse histories. They are able to share their feelings in an Alcoholics Anonymous support group or other support groups for recovering alcoholics, such as Women for Sobriety. This one-on-one sharing and connecting among adult survivors may be enough for them to break through their isolation and shame concerning the abuse. Most can more readily benefit from a self-help group dedicated specifically to the needs of abuse survivors, and/or from individual therapy. We will look at these choices more completely in Chapter Twelve.

Remember that *both* the alcoholism and the sexual abuse need to be treated, that dealing with one doesn't make the other disappear. I think it is most necessary to first deal with the alcoholism; sobriety is helpful in giving survivors the strength to also deal successfully with their sexual abuse.

Alcoholism and Active Sexual Behavior

Many female alcoholics who were sexually abused as children may be sexually active with numerous partners. They falsely learned through childhood sexual abuse that being sexual was a way to get affection, have worth, and gain power, even though it may have filled them with self-loathing at the same time. It's possible that their active sexual behavior is a way of expressing anger at men in general, and the abuser in particular, for the abuse they experienced as children. All of this may lead them to seek out superficial sexual encounters as a way to feel powerful and not victimized. Add in the dynamic of abuse destroying personal boundaries, which results in survivors being taught they have no right to say no, and the stage is set for continuing sexual misery.

Be Compassionate with Yourself

If you see yourself in this category, try to be understanding and compassionate about your active sexual behavior.

The last thing you need is to feel like an awful person. You were just trying to cope with what happened to you as a child and to get your needs met in the way you learned how.

When achieving and maintaining sobriety, many alcoholic adult survivors adopt a radically different outlook on sexuality. A significant number of them choose to not be sexual. The same decision is sometimes made by nonalcoholic survivors who, early on, choose to deny their sexuality and never have an active sexual life. Whether an adult survivor chooses to have sexual relationships or not, part of recovery is learning how to have safe, respectful, caring, and nonabusive friendships. Adult survivors need to know the signs of healthy and nonabusive friendships.

Fear of sexuality doesn't have to be a permanent state of affairs. The fear is quite natural, in a sense, for survivors may not have *ever* been sexual with anyone while they were sober. They need to give themselves permission not to be in a sexual relationship until they feel they are ready. Talking with a therapist or sharing their fears, concerns, and memories with a support group or friends can help these women come to terms with difficult sexual feelings.

THE CAUSES OF DUAL ABUSE IN FAMILIES

When sexual abuse takes place, it's because there is a breakdown in the function of the family. This usually means the parents aren't protecting, caring for, and nurturing their children. The same sort of breakdown happens in a family where one or both parents are alcoholic. Members of both types of families don't get their emotional and nurturing needs met. There is also an inevitable confusion of generational boundaries as children end up feeling responsible for — and yet, unsafe around — alcoholic parents. People don't talk about feelings and often "explode" or become verbally or physically abusive to family members. Other families keep all their emotions and feelings pent up inside, while pretending everything is wonderful to the outside world.

Both sexually abusive and alcoholic family systems have very active denial systems regarding their real problems. If children are abused, sexually or otherwise, they already know they must keep their silence about it. These families are extremely rigid, closed, and secretive systems that are isolated from the community, and yet keep a pretense of solidarity to outsiders.

Most people have at times had feelings of wanting to call others names and be verbally abusive. And who among us hasn't occasionally wanted to hit or shove someone who angered us? It's even quite normal to sometimes feel sexually attracted toward others with whom it would be inappropriate to be sexual, such as siblings, or a friend's spouse or lover. These feelings can even exist between parents and children. But *having* these fleeting feelings and choosing to *act* on them are completely different things. We are each responsible to make appropriate choices and to not act on inappropriate feelings. And that is where the line between abuser and nonabuser is drawn.

Alcoholism Is Conducive to Abuse

In a family where personal boundaries are already blurred, such as a family where there is alcoholism, the risk is greater that someone with sexual feelings toward a child or toward another person with whom sexual activity would be inappropriate will ignore societal sanctions and cross over the boundary into sexual behavior that is inappropriate and abusive. The use of alcohol or other drugs can play an important role in triggering such abusive events by lowering inhibitions. Alcoholism doesn't cause childhood sexual abuse, but it certainly plays a part in creating an atmosphere where such abuse is more easily tolerated and rationalized.

Because of the blurring of personal boundaries, the alcoholic family system leaves the door open for sexual abuse to take place either inside or outside the family. In alcoholic family systems where there is no sexual abuse by either parent, there is a greater danger of siblings being sexually abusive to other siblings. There is also a hazard of sexual abuse being inflicted on the children by persons outside the immediate family, such as uncles, grandparents, cousins, or neighborhood teens and adults. This increased vulnerability happens for a number of reasons:

- In a family where one or both parents are alcoholic, the parents are apt to be emotionally distant from their children, rather than giving them the love and attention they need. This makes the children easier prey to others — inside or outside the family — who may give them the attention they want — only in abusive ways. Remember, children may be unable to distinguish between good and hurtful attention. And they usually don't feel free to go to their emotionally distant parents to tell them of any hurts or episodes of confusing touches.
- These families produce fuzzy and inappropriate boundaries regarding proper relationships between the parents and the children. The children aren't sure where their rights stop and other people's rights begin. This sort of confusion makes it harder for the children to say no to people, even if they feel they are asked to do something wrong.
- In these families, the children are used to seeing the alcoholic model behavior that is tyrannizing and controlling toward other members of the family. The nonalcoholic parent may also be very controlling. Children who have been made to feel constantly fearful at home will be just as afraid of and as easily intimidated by people outside the home.

YOU DON'T HAVE TO REPEAT YOUR FAMILY SCRIPT

Almost all children from families where there is alcoholism and sexual abuse, whether they are direct victims of the abuse or not, suffer some form of emotional neglect while growing up. But it doesn't follow that you are doomed to repeat the family script you grew up with. In fact, most adult survivors will not sexually or physically abuse their children. But many will be emotionally distant from their children and may find it difficult to adequately bond with them. At times they may also be verbally and emotionally abusive to the children, even though they don't want to do so. It is what they have learned. Some women may unwittingly marry a sexual abuser and/or alcoholic because the personality type feels so comfortable and familiar to them. After all, it's what they grew up with.

Your Blueprint for a Better Future

As you enter your recovery from childhood sexual abuse, you regain your power to have choices. You may wish to explore your family blueprint — a set of behaviors, rules, and attitudes that has been passed down from generation to generation. The term *blueprint* seems accurate to me, because blueprints can be revised. You can redraw self-destructive and outmoded blueprints, changing them so that you can design a better life for yourself and for your own family.

Families *can* be safe and loving. Families can respect one another's rights and boundaries from person to person and from generation to generation. Families can express feelings and learn how to resolve conflict. The recovery process can change family blueprints and can stop the cycles of sexual abuse and alcoholism. There is hope for a better future through your making peace with and understanding the past.

Dealing with Your Childhood Family

Adult survivors of families where alcohol is abused may want to work through their sexual abuse issues with the families. Unfortunately, they may find the going tough. In many cases, their families may not — in the depths of their denial — even acknowledge there is anything to *discuss*. That's all the more reason for adult survivors to take their recovery in their own hands. Even though they may want to explore family counseling, they should not expect much help and support from those family members who abused them. For those lucky enough to get support from within their families, it can be a great help, but it isn't *necessary* for their healing process.

It's important to always remember that alcoholic adult abusers committing sexual abuse while drinking *are* responsible for the abuse they inflict. It's no different from running someone down with a car while drunk. A sexual abuser is responsible for his or her sexual violations of another person's physical and psychological boundaries.

If you suffer from a history that includes both alcoholism and childhood sexual abuse, you will need to deal with both problems to become the whole person you deserve to be. It may be helpful for you to remember that working on one will help you deal with the other.

Sobriety alone won't remove the pain of your childhood sexual abuse, just as coming to terms with the abuse and its effects won't give you sobriety. But sobriety *will* start you connecting with other people in the most healing, loving ways possible. And as you heal from childhood sexual abuse and realize your worth as a person and as an adult survivor, you will learn to accept yourself, full of understanding for your past and hope for the future.

CHAPTER EIGHT

YOU, AS A PARENT TO YOUR CHILDREN

Adult survivors of childhood sexual abuse worry a lot about their own parenting skills. Some are afraid of becoming parents and passing the abuse on, while those who already are parents often express a desire to "be a different and better parent than what I had." Both groups worry that the incidents of sexual abuse in their childhoods, and the under-nurturing and chaos in their parental families, may affect their own parenting. They want to protect their children from sexual abuse without making them paranoid. They want their children to like themselves. They want to know how to talk to their children about sex and their bodies without making them shameful — the way these parents were made to feel.

If you share in these fears and these desires to find a better way of raising a family, that's a healthy sign. It *is* true that much of what we learn about how to parent comes from how we were parented. But that does not mean you will be like your parents, especially if you understand the dynamics of your abuse and consciously work at learning new ways to parent that are more consistent and nurturing than what you experienced.

PARENTING ISSUES ADULT SURVIVORS FACE

Some adult survivors say they are afraid to tell people they've been sexually abused because they fear people will automatically think they've been sexually abusing their own children.

Some women survivors of childhood sexual abuse are concerned — because of their background of being abused — about being sexually inappropriate with their children or about picking a mate who might abuse their children. A woman I'll call Anna related these feelings:

> *I really fly off the handle and get very out of control with my kids at times. I love them very much, and basically I think I'm a good mother, but it's hard for me not to blame them sometimes and not be verbally abusive when my life gets too frustrating. When I can't control my anger like that and I take it out on the kids, I sound so much like my dad, and it scares the hell out of me. I don't want to be like him in any way.*

If you struggle with parenting issues as an adult survivor, you aren't alone. Even if you haven't been verbally or physically abusive to your children, you may have unclear boundaries. You may be emotionally more distant than you want and have difficulty showing your children affection. Or perhaps you expect them to act too old for their age, and you try to share your adult concerns and problems with them. Or you may be inconsistent: sometimes too rigid and strict, followed by periods of "anything goes" permissiveness. These are all common parenting traits of women who were sexually abused as children. But you can change these traits and your children can benefit very much from all the positive changes you make in your behavior.

You can further make changes by disarming the power of the behavior patterns of the family you grew up in. Look at ways you may be like your parents — even abusing or alcoholic parents. We all learn behaviors from our parents, even ones we disliked. Your parents may have yelled often and been verbally abusive, and you hated it. But you may find yourself angry often. One of your parents may have been controlling, sarcastic, passive, alcoholic, and so on. It can be helpful, if you're willing, to say, "I do some of those same things, and I don't like it. I don't want to be anything like them." Admitting that you behave in ways you feel are unacceptable gives you more power to change your behavior and to get help if it's needed, particularly if it hurts your children and your relationship with them.

Adult Survivors Can Be Better Parents

One of the most helpful things you can do to be a good parent is to continue healing from your past and becoming a competent, happy adult, living in the present. Children are very creative and adaptable; your kids will change in response to your changes. Children learn mostly from our examples, *not* from what we say. If, for example, you want your children to learn to not be so serious and to be more playful, the best thing you can do is to take time to play with them, and to let them see you being playful with your friends or mate.

Parenting is a skill that will never be perfect, but it can be learned and fine-tuned at any age. Here are some basic guidelines for parenting a healthy family:

Take Care of Yourself

Do not get your primary needs — such as companionship, affection, and support — met through your children. You are an adult and those needs will best be met through the time you spend with other adults. Also, there are times *you* need to come first, and your children need to learn that. We all need time alone, time to just be with ourselves. It can be helpful to use this time alone to reflect, to meditate, and to give ourselves affirmations regarding the positive things in our life.

Have a Good Network of Friends

Again, don't rely on your children to be your confidantes. You need to spend time with adults who relate to you, are sympathetic, and with whom you can have fun.

Develop Loving Communication with Your Significant Other

The best way to teach children is through example. Children will learn to enjoy life more and to appreciate other people if they see their parents model loving and caring feelings toward each other and other people.

Be Loving and Affirming with Your Children

It's difficult to do this *all* the time, but you can make it an important part of your everyday life by consciously striving to do things such as the following:

- Regularly tell your kids you love them.
- Regularly give them hugs.
- Don't make fun of them.
- Don't call them negative names.
- Don't hit or shove them.
- Don't yell at them.
- Encourage their expression of feelings.

Build Consistency and Structure

Try to be consistent in your love and behavior toward your kids. *This makes them feel loved and safe.* Provide rules and consequences. *This gives them the sense of security and freedom they need to grow within healthy limits.* Rules and consequences minimize fighting and blaming because parents and children then know what is expected and what happens when rules aren't followed. Allow some flexibility for special events in a child's life, but for the most part, consistency provides security.

When You Make a Mistake or Yell at a Child, Apologize

Let your children see that you are human and can make mistakes. Let them also see that it's okay to apologize, to admit when you are wrong. If you find yourself yelling at your children — which can be frightening to them — apologize immediately. The most helpful way to break a hurtful cycle is to apologize and ask your children to tell you if you hurt them, explaining that yelling is wrong.

Let Your Children See that You Are Human and Have Feelings

This will give them permission to have feelings too. You can have your feelings and not burden your children. You can be mad at a child and state your anger without screaming, or using put-downs. You can be mad at a child and still let the child know you love him or her.

Don't Burden Your Children

Don't burden children with your adult problems, but let them know what is going on in a way they can understand at their age. For example, tell them that you had a hard day at work, but also let them know you don't expect them to solve the problem for you. This will help them know why you are upset, but that you're not upset with them.

Share Your Views About Life and Spirituality

Don't feel embarrassed to talk about your personal beliefs and feelings. Children need a foundation in life's meanings, hopes, and spiritual values through home teaching, in addition to outside instruction they may get through school or organized religion.

Talk to Your Children About Their Sexuality and Their Developing Bodies

In order to feel good about their bodies and their sexuality, children need ongoing openness — with appropriate boundaries. They need to feel good about being a boy or girl. They need to know their bodies are their own and that they have the right to privacy (within age guidelines) and the right to say no if someone touches or restrains them in a way they don't like. Children may not, for example, want to hug Uncle Ned who has a scratchy beard, or they may be afraid of someone with a loud voice or a mannerism they shy away from. They should never be forced to hug, kiss, or show affection when they don't want to. In fact, they should be asked. For example, instead of saying, ''Now you be a good girl and kiss Grandpa good-night,'' try saying, ''Do you want to kiss Grandpa good-night?'' Let them make the decision.

Separate Their Behavior from Them

This is very important. Let children know when you don't like what they're doing. But don't say they are a bad boy or girl for doing it. Don't say, ''You're bad for writing on the wall.'' This is guaranteed to shame them. Say instead, ''I do not like it when you write on the wall; please don't do it or I'll put your colors away.'' Or, ''It is not okay to hit your sister, so go to your room and come back when you want to make up.'' Always give them a way to come back and join the group. And never equate bad behavior with being a bad person.

Children Are Not Small Adults

One of the most significant things for all parents to remember is that children are children — they're not small adults. You shouldn't attribute adult intelligence or malice to their behavior, no matter how bright they are. Children can be devious, and they will sometimes push limits as far as they can. But they are usually doing so to discover what the limits of their lives and their powers are.

Avoid Verbal and Physical Abuse

Hitting, screaming, swearing, and name-calling are all examples of being out of control, being abusive. If you grew up with abuse in your family, your parents' and sometimes your siblings' behavior was probably out of control. So to you, such behavior may seem familiar, though almost all survivors say it doesn't feel good inside when they behave that way. You may honestly feel that yelling and physical roughness are a good way to make a point. Ask yourself this question: If you were having trouble understanding something or were just plain afraid of a certain project, or you made a mistake at work, would getting verbally abused or physically struck help you understand or perform better? Of course it wouldn't. And it won't help your children either.

ARE YOU CONCERNED ABOUT POSSIBLE SEXUAL ABUSE OF YOUR CHILDREN?

If you have any concerns about possible sexual abuse taking place, ask your child or teen about it, but do not ask in an alarming way. Sit down with young children and see if they know the difference between "good touch" and "bad touch." Explain the difference. There are many good books on the topic; one is *Red Flag, Green Flag People,* a coloring book published by the Crisis Center in Fargo, North Dakota.

What follows is a simplified listing of examples of good and bad touch, which is found in *Red Flag, Green Flag People.* Good touch can be such things as

- a hug from Dad,
- a kiss from Mom,
- holding hands with a friend at school,
- a pat on the back for a job well done.

Some examples of bad touch include when

- someone hits you,
- someone pinches you or tickles you when you don't like it,
- someone touches your private parts,
- someone touches you when you don't want the person to.

It helps for all parents to educate their children as a precautionary measure. If you ask children to list their own examples of good and bad touch after you've explained the difference, they usually catch on very quickly.

Once they have this basic understanding, you can ask them if anyone has touched them using bad touch. Be sure to let them know that they can come to you and tell you about it. Tell them you will do something about it, no matter who touched them and how they may have been threatened. Also let them know you won't be upset with them, that you love them no matter what. Then, if it turns out that sexual abuse may have taken place, follow through with the appropriate steps of calling a child protection agency or another agency that works with victims of abuse. You can get help in dealing with both the legal and the emotional sides of caring for your child.

What follows are guidelines for preventing sexual abuse to your children.

Don't Treat Children Like Miniature Adults

Children should not be treated as little adults. Gaining a thorough knowledge of children's developmental stages will help you determine what is appropriate behavior and treatment toward your children. Single parents need to be sensitive to the tendency to share too much with their children when there is no other adult in the household to share their adult feelings and concerns with.

Children Have Rights

Teach your children that they have the right to be assertive, to loudly say "no" to people who tell or ask them to do things they feel are wrong. It's their right to be protected from abuse, and they need to know they are free to come and tell you anything.

Set Boundaries

Boundaries need to be established between children, children and older siblings, and children and adults. Make sure the rules of respecting each other's privacy and boundaries are known by all family members and are expected to be followed.

Encourage Open Expression of Feelings

All family members need to know that it is okay to openly express their feelings. Open expression makes it hard for any family member to exploit other family members in any way, including sexually abusing them.

Good Partner Relationship

Clear communication between parents, giving and receiving nurturing from one another, the capacity to have fun together, and to relate sexually as adults all help prevent the formation of an abusive family atmosphere.

Open Discussion of Appropriate Sexuality Information

Talk with your children about sexuality and their bodies. Have age-appropriate books and information at home.

Non-Sexual Hugging and Touching Among Family Members

This includes open communication so that your children are able to tell you *anything*. It also includes non-sexual ways to show affection, and ways to spend time together that are fun for both parent and child.

It's important that you teach children to be physically close and show physical affection without being sexual.

Adequate Privacy

Rules providing for adequate and age-appropriate privacy for dressing, bathing, and for sexual matters should be formed for and understood by all family members. Even young pre-schoolers will ask for privacy to master their toilet needs. We wouldn't let a three-year-old lock the door, but we can let him or her close it while we wait outside in case help is needed.

Teach About Sexual Abuse

Read books and teach the whole family about good touch and bad touch as a way to promote understanding and prevention of childhood sexual abuse. *When children are well educated on the subject, they are not so vulnerable to abuse.*

We can all use more information and education to be better parents. We need support and communication with other parents to check things out and bounce around ideas. Situations regularly come up for all parents where they can benefit from a discussion with others who are going through similar experiences.

Single Parents

If you're a single parent, you deal with the same stresses that all couples deal with, and then some. It is especially important for you to get adequate support from friends and other parents. Remember, you don't have to be perfect or know everything there is to know about parenting. There is an entire world of other parents to help you, plus there are excellent books, and some first-rate parenting classes available all around the country. So don't keep yourself isolated with uncertainty and doubts. Reach out and do what you must to be the kind of parent that will help your children grow into healthy adults.

Parents Anonymous

If you are at the breaking point and feel a strong urge to verbally or physically abuse your children, leave the room for a moment. Try to cool down, count to ten, call a friend or an abuse hot line. If you have recurrent concerns about losing control with your children and possibly hurting them, even after talking to friends or counselors, then you need further support. Parents Anonymous is a national self-help group for parents who are afraid they might abuse or have already verbally or physically abused their children. A Parents Anonymous number should be listed in your local telephone directory. You can also call your local child protection agency, especially if you fear for your children's safety.

As children who were abused, adult survivors were treated as adults by being given too much responsibility for and knowledge of adult concerns. Hence, they may have more trouble setting their own children's limits. Most children don't really begin to have adult intelligence — the ability to fully examine two sides of a complex issue and make judgments — until mid-teens, and even then they lack the years of life experience necessary to totally reason as an adult. Talk to other parents, take a class, or read some books on child development so you know what to expect from your kids and what their limits are. Then you're still going to need a truckload of patience, but that's what parenting is all about.

CHAPTER NINE

SEXUALITY

A realistic and holistic view of sex should go beyond the merely physical to include everything you think, feel, and do related to yourself as a female sexual being. Your sexuality both affects and is in turn affected by all aspects of your life, including your female self-esteem. So let's look at sexuality as consisting of three areas:

1. Beliefs, attitudes, and values
2. Feelings
3. Physical behaviors

MAKING YOUR OWN RULES

Our beliefs and attitudes about ourselves as women — and sexual beings — come from all we have learned about women and sex from our families, friends, the church, the media, and other sources. Sexuality is mostly comprised of our beliefs and feelings and is less concerned with the act of being sexual. In other words, it's important for you to determine the attitudes and rules governing your sexuality so you can make a conscious decision whether or not they are good for you.

Traditionally, either the church, the family, the mass media, or men have defined how women are supposed to look, act, and think. They have also laid out women's roles as females, wives, and mothers. Almost every female in this country has experienced the hurts and pains of sexism, whether it is from feeling inferior because of growing up in a culture that said men could do more and have more freedom and more worth, or simply from the relentless media portrayal of women as sex objects. We are saturated and over-whelmed — often without knowing it — by the media's view of what it means to be a sexual woman: perfumed, alarm-ingly thin, dressed in high fashion and high heels, always willing, and totally orgasmic. We may become so uncon-sciously guided by these images that we try to re-create ourselves to imitate them. And in doing so, we ignore the opportunity of finding out what we may find sexual or sexually stimulating to ourselves. If we accept others' definitions of what it means to be a sexual woman, we forfeit the chance to define the meaning for ourselves.

Stereotypes Abound

Despite some progress, the same stereotypes are still around. For example, some people believe that girls and women are responsible for causing their own rapes by stimulating or inviting the rapist's sexual feelings: "She was asking for it." In such a case, in 1984, a Wisconsin judge gave a convicted rapist a lenient sentence and characterized the *six-year-old* female victim as a very seductive young lady. The outrage this miscarriage of justice generated didn't begin to make up for the judge's total lack of understanding and compassion regarding women and their sexuality, children and the subject of sexual abuse, or of a rapist's responsibility for his sexual actions.

In loving families, females get validated for their worth as individuals and are somewhat buffered from society's relentless sex stereotyping. But for children who are sexually abused by a family member, the family is not a protector, but the primary source of their wounds.

MESSAGES CHILDHOOD SEXUAL ABUSE GIVES

All women from inconsistent, undernurturing families, whether they are sexually abused or not, will benefit from identifying negative and false attitudes about sexuality that they received from their families.

Sexual Worth

If the father, or a father figure, pays particular attention to a young girl in sexual ways — the extreme being sexual intercourse — then that is how she will likely determine her worth to men. It is closely tied to her physical expression of sexuality.

Confusing Sexuality with Closeness

When children are sexually abused, they learn to connect in sexual ways. Again, if that is how they got special attention — perhaps the only times they received *any* attention — they learn to relate to others sexually and thus confuse being close to someone with being sexual. Many of these children go on to be very sexually active teenagers and adults. It is their way to get attention and love; it is a way to have power and be important. And it may be the only way they know to be close to another person.

Can't Say No to Sex

When sexual boundaries are violated, children learn they have no rights. For many this sets up a pattern of feeling that as adults they have no right to say no to a sexual partner, whether the partner is male or female. The intense feelings

97

or powerlessness resulting from this behavior inevitably makes them feel very resentful toward their partners.

Some adult survivors of childhood sexual abuse react by avoiding dating altogether. Some even refuse to be alone with a man — they so fear being unable to say no if sexually approached.

Reactive and Caretaking Behavior

Children who were abused become skilled at anticipating — and reacting to — the behavior of their parents and other family members. These behaviors were developed as a way for the children to cope — during the time they were abused — with the horrible reality of that abuse. If they knew the abuse was coming, they could prepare themselves for it in some way, perhaps by dissociating or by trying to look unattractive. Some survivors carry these "anticipating" behaviors into their adult lives at the expense of their own best interests. This sort of behavior is called *caretaking behavior*. It is also often called *codependency*. It means that you live your life for other people; you focus on them instead of yourself. You develop the behavior because

- you may have been taught or exploited as a child to fulfill others' needs. In doing so, you've learned your own needs are not important.
- the undernurturing family system has taught you to *please* people so you can earn or win love and approval.
- you may have thought as a child that if you were *very* good, you might avoid the worst of the abuse.

Mixed Messages

Many abused children get the message that says "bad" girls are sexual and "good" girls aren't. This message comes from many sources, including Mom, the church, and perhaps even the abuser. How devastated and confused girls must get when a caregiver figure like Dad gives them the message that good girls aren't sexual and yet he or someone else is being sexual with them. This mixed message also means that bad girls get the attention and good girls don't. A girl child in a family where abuse occurs is then left with a lose-lose situation. She either feels shameful and bad *and* gets attention, or she is a "good girl" and gets ignored and rejected by Dad and later on, she fears, by all boys. Some fathers actually tell their young daughters, "I wouldn't do this with your mom (or your sister) because she's too pure, too Christian, or too frigid."

The Media's Influence

All women get these messages from the media: Your body needs to look a certain way — big breasts, small waist, or thin thighs — the list is endless. Young girls and teens are diagnosed with eating disorders at near epidemic proportions. These eating disorders are connected, at least in part, to the pervasive influence of the media. The result is girls believe that to be loved, they must have a specific physical appearance.

Men Are More Valued, Have More Power

Since men are more often the ones who violate children sexually, they exert power and control over the children in extreme ways. To victims of childhood sexual abuse, the men may seem to occupy a position of great power. The mothers in abusive families are usually passive when the father is around, but may later take their anger and frustrations out on their children.

Masturbation Is Bad

Many women survivors believe that masturbation is wrong or disgusting. In families where there is abuse, sexuality is usually very repressed, making everything connected with it seem shameful. Masturbation can be an expression of healthy sexuality; yet, since most adult survivors have experienced inappropriate fondling and touching, touching themselves in masturbation and the shame surrounding their abuse can easily become mixed up.

Men Are Stereotyped Too

The bit of sexist folklore that says females are responsible for the arousal of men's sexual feelings also says that if a woman is raped, she asked for it: she dressed in a provocative manner, she was a tease, and so on. But men are not the enemy. Men are stereotyped, too, because this myth also implies that men are out of control like wild animals. Men in general are not the enemy, and it is not helpful for you to see them as such. You may be mad at some men in your life — and justifiably so — but it is a mistake and not helpful to you to make this a universal feeling about all men.

VALIDATING OUR FEELINGS

It is important to know yourself and what you are feeling. Feelings are bits of emotional information that can help you decide how you want to fulfill your needs. For example, if you're feeling lonely, you might want to see a friend, and you may say you need a hug. If you feel sexual, you may want to be sexual in some manner, but you may not. If you're feeling hungry, you can eat. Feelings are not good or bad, per se. They just *are*. The important thing for you to remember is that you can choose whether or not to act on them.

Women who were abused, particularly incest victims, feel a lot of shame about their sexuality. It's important that they let go of the shame, guilt, and responsibility for their sexual abuse and put the responsibility back on the abuser. Many women not only carry shame for being childhood victims of incest, but they feel a double shame for having responded sexually during the abuse, perhaps even enjoying the physical sensations of sexual touching — a natural enough response. This is very common. Most adult survivors, when they feel safe, acknowledge having felt some physical pleasure during the abusive episodes. Bodies tend to respond to touch, even when the touch is forced or bribed in some way — just as all of us might respond to tickling by laughing, no matter who is tickling us or whether or not we want to be tickled.

Promiscuity

Another source of shame for some abuse survivors comes from being sexually active as teenagers or adults. This, too, is common behavior in survivors. Remember, it's how they learned to get attention and "love." Many sexual abuse survivors learned validation and personal power through being sexual. Promiscuity is a misguided search to find love, nurturing, and acceptance — and it doesn't work. For this reason, women need to learn to differentiate between needs that nurture and needs that are purely sexual.

Abstaining from Sexual Behavior

On the other side of the promiscuity coin are the sexual abuse survivors who choose not to be sexual. It's probably not a conscious choice for many of them, but for some it is. They may see abstaining from sexual behavior as a way to stay safe — to prevent people from having power over them. They believe they can best stay safe and maintain their boundaries by not being sexual with anyone. Since viewpoints often are all-or-none in families where abuse occurs, it follows that if women from such families allow others to be sexual with them, they lose their power or control. They may feel shameful that they are different and not sexual, but they are willing to pay that price for feeling safer. Others may want a sexual relationship, but repeatedly sabotage the possibility because they are too frightened of the possible consequences. Lesbian survivors, as all survivors, will struggle with their fears of being intimate, manipulated, sexually vulnerable, as well as needing to separate abuse issues from healthy, loving relationships.

Affirming your self-esteem can be one of the most healing and satisfying processes involved with recovering from childhood sexual abuse. It is important to

- understand how natural it is for a child to respond to the "attention" of abuse by thinking that being sexual is a good way to be close to people.
- understand and forgive yourself if your body responded sexually to the touching.
- forgive yourself and have compassion for yourself as the teenager or young adult who may have been promiscuous while looking for affection and acceptance.
- forgive yourself if you were sexual with younger children during your youth.

If you were sexual with younger children, you were repeating behavior that was taught to you. For most people in recovery, it is important to eventually seek out those children they were sexual with as youths and apologize and be open to giving them any details they may need to deal with the abuse.

But that was then, and this is now. Now *you* can set your own boundaries and rules for being sexual. The number one rule is the one that says *you* always have the right and the responsibility to say no to any sexual involvement if it is not what you desire.

CHOOSING YOUR BEHAVIOR

Act Responsibly

Sexuality is a health issue. You have a responsibility to take care of yourself and to have regular pelvic exams. If you are uncomfortable seeing a male doctor, you don't have to. There are more female doctors and nurse practitioners today than ever before. You need to learn about how AIDS and venereal diseases are contracted, and you need to know about birth control and how to have safe sex. Learn how your body works and understand what a miracle it is. The more you know, the better you will take care of yourself, emotionally and physically.

Be True to Yourself

Being physically sexual is actually a very small part of sexuality, but it is still important. It is a very fun, enjoyable, and special intimate activity. When you make good, deliberate choices about your partner and about when and where you want to be sexual, it can be one of the most fulfilling physical and emotional experiences in life. But, if you don't make deliberate choices or don't feel you have that right, being sexual can turn into pain, shame, anger, and can feel abusive. Working out the issues of your childhood sexual abuse will help take the pain away from your sexuality.

John Brantner, who taught at the University of Minnesota, made the following list of eight components that go into being intimate and sexual with another person. Think about how these components fit into your ideas of intimacy and sexuality.

1. Equality in status
2. Desire to love
3. Experience of affection
4. Search for closeness

5. Willingness to be vulnerable
6. Commitment to understanding another person
7. Loyalty and exclusivity
8. Courage to be sexual

TAKING RESPONSIBILITY
IN A SEXUAL RELATIONSHIP

Know Yourself Sexually

Become acquainted with your body, your likes and dislikes. Identify what qualities or activities turn you on and what turns you off when you spend time with your partner. These are usually very subjective things, but I've listed some common to many women — add your own likes and dislikes to the lists.

Turn-ons: Romance, showers, vacations, poetry, good conversation, deep emotional conversations, dressing up, sports, laughter, a cozy fire, a secluded cabin, sensuous fabrics, a warm bubble bath, beautiful music, or a walk in the rain.

Turn-offs: Bad breath, body odor, force, anger, tension, dirty fingernails, inattention to what is being said, wanting just sex and nothing else, self-centeredness, disregard for others' feelings, or a TV playing in the background.

Communicate with Your Partner

Talk — show your partner what you like sexually. Learn to talk about your sexual wants and needs, as well as your other physical or emotional needs and desires. At first, it may feel foreign, but any change in behavior takes time to feel natural.

Listen to your partner, but learn not to take things totally personally. For example, if your partner doesn't want to be sexual when you want to, it doesn't mean there is something wrong with you. Think of it this way: if you fixed a sandwich for your significant other and he or she wasn't hungry and couldn't eat, would you take it as a personal slight? It's the same when it comes to being sexual — the right to say no belongs to everybody.

Be Responsible to, Not for Your Partner

You're not responsible to know your partner's needs and desires *before* they are communicated. You are, however, accountable to listen and honestly attempt to understand those wants and needs when they *are* communicated. Most times, people can compromise on their wants and needs. But first, it's important that you are true to yourself, even though you may want to take some initiative in learning what pleases your partner.

Don't Make Assumptions

Check out your feelings with your partner. Many times we get hurt over an imagined affront. Also, most of us are at our most vulnerable when we're sexual with others. Make sure you are with someone you trust and be willing to be open about your feelings. Remember, your partner isn't a mind reader and can't care for your feelings before you make them clear.

Acceptance

Be honest and open with your partner, but also be willing to accept that, at various times, your partner will have different needs and different wants than you do. You need to be accepting and caring; don't judge one another. Allow the differences between you to exist, and decide for yourself, in a nonjudgmental way, whether they are things you can accept.

FLASHBACKS AND DESENSITIZATION STEPS

Being sexual with a partner doesn't have to trigger flashbacks and memories of sexual abuse. You can use these suggestions to eliminate or at least move toward controlling and eventually eliminating flashbacks:

- Know your partner well enough so you can talk about your past abuse and the problem of recurring memories. You will need to ask for support from your partner.
- Start by taking a break from being sexual and take some weeks — or even months if you need them — to be held at night and get hugs. Know that for now this is your limit. Pay attention to when you want affection and when you don't. Ask to stop being physical if you feel uncomfortable with what is happening. You need to know you are in charge of choosing when you want to be physical or sexual.
- When you feel you are ready to be sexual, remind yourself and your partner that you may need to stop at any time if it becomes scary to you. If you stop because what you are doing is triggering a flashback, remind yourself that what you are feeling is a memory of the past — that you're in the present, an adult, and the past can't hurt you as it did. If you feel comfortable, you may want to resume your actions.

These suggestions will eventually help you to (1) feel in charge of your sexuality and not feel victimized, and (2) separate the memories of the past from what is happening in the present.

Once abuse survivors start talking to their partners and know they have a right to say they don't want to be sexual or to ask them to refrain from doing something that is a flashback trigger, their ability to be sexually intimate can begin to dramatically improve. And remember, if you don't know your partner well enough to talk about your sexual abuse background and your fears and feelings about sex, then perhaps you don't know him or her well enough to be sexual.

There's a big difference between a dating situation and a long-term relationship. You may not want to share much of your past with a new partner at first. Some women have told too much about their abuse to a new partner, only to have it used against them in put-downs. So, it's generally a good idea to make decisions slowly about what to share, when to share it, and with whom. Go slow and establish a sense of trust that is comfortable for you.

IMPROVING YOUR SEXUALITY
AND YOUR FEMALE SELF-ESTEEM

Think about the information and attitudes you picked up about being female and remember *where* you learned them. Share these with some women friends to help you sort out your underlying beliefs about yourself as a female. Revise those rules and attitudes that you disagree with and that hold you back from living and enjoying your life and sexuality to the fullest. Remember, the rules are *yours*, and you have the right to revise them anytime, as often as you choose. You have the right to feel good about your body and yourself as a woman and a person. It is a helpful exercise to replace negative messages you received about your sexuality with positive ones. Below is a list of affirmations that you can give to yourself. Feel free to create your own as well, and make them applicable to your own unique life and viewpoint.

Affirmations for Sexuality

- *It's wonderful to be female!*
- *I am lovable.*
- *My sexual needs are okay.*
- *I have a right to ask for what I want sexually.*
- *My body is muscular and likes to run and play hard.*
- *I am a complete sexual person.*
- *I am not perfect. I am okay.*
- *I can be cuddled and not be sexual.*

- *Sexual fantasies and feelings are okay. I can choose to act on these feelings or not.*
- *It's okay to be where I am.*
- *I am exploring my sexuality and it's fun.*

Use these affirmations in your daily life. Write one for each day and carry it with you. Say one or more aloud to yourself during the day. These nurturing affirmations will become more natural to you each day that you use them.

Your Body Image

Look at your nude body in the mirror. This is *your* body, and you don't have to listen to anybody else about how it should look. You have a right and responsibility to know your body physically. It is healthy to know your body so you can feel good and normal about it, but also to spot any changes that may be medically important for your physician to know.

Look at your nude body nonjudgmentally.

- Take note of such features as whether you are short, tall, long-legged, or short-waisted.
- Note any scars from surgery, birthmarks, or stretch marks from childbirth.
- Thank your body for how long it has been with you and how loyally it has served you all these years.
- Tell your body aloud that you welcome and accept it just as it is.

Look at your genitals in a mirror. This is something that most women have never done and I think it is indicative of the shame that gets perpetuated around female genitals — their "uncleanliness" and the "disgust" and "sinfulness" connected with sexuality and masturbation. Look at yourself and try to accept what you see as another wonder of nature. Why is it that men get to brag about their genitals while many women seem to feel shameful about theirs? Remember, the more you know about your body and see it for the beautifully designed and super-efficient biological wonder it is, the more natural and accepting you will feel of it.

Enjoy and Take Care of Your Body

Start to feel better about your body by keeping it in shape and pampering it through exercise, massage, dance, or bubble baths. Appreciate how your body works. Let yourself visualize the muscles shaping and flexing. Be thankful to your body for being your companion all these years, for taking you where you've wanted to go, through all the illnesses and injuries you've been through together. Remember that your physical self needs to be tended to and nurtured just as your emotional self and your spiritual self do.

Enjoying and becoming more aware of your physical self can also heighten your awareness of your sensual and sexual experiences. Allow yourself to have your sexual feelings and fantasies without judging them. We need to take responsibility for whether we act on those feelings or not, but it is very natural to have them.

Take a self-defense class, or yoga, or dance, or anything else that will make you pay attention to your body and how it works. Many of these classes are now being taught to women with twofold purposes:

1. To help them discover that they can have the physical strength and expertise to take care of themselves.
2. To help them develop the self-confidence that will carry over into other areas, making it less likely that they will again be prey to an abusive situation.

Classes such as these are a way of feeling more in touch with your own body and feeling empowered in your life.

Mothers and Daughters

Your mother was your first and most likely your primary model for what an adult female should be like. She gave you your basic attitudes about women. Many women from abusive family systems, especially where there's strong attachments, have a lot of guilt about pulling away from the family ideas of what roles a female should play. The guilt comes from strong feelings of loyalty toward their mother. Many women feel guilty saying anything negative about their mothers or trying to live their lives differently from their mothers. The more rigid your family was and the more insecure Mom is, the less she may be able to tolerate your being different without feeling hurt. Many lesbian women, or women who have a mate without marriage or a baby, may be rejected because they are straying from the family blueprint of what is acceptable. If you fall into any of these categories, you need to remember that this issue is about *your family's* rigidity and insecurity, not about you.

Ask your mother what messages she got from her parental family about women and their sexuality. This is usually an experience that connects mothers and daughters. It may well be the first time that both of you have connected together as adult women, sharing personally with one another. It usually helps to develop more acceptance of your mother, and it may lead to an understanding of why she "couldn't" have acted differently when you were growing up. Most importantly, it will help you see that the abuse wasn't your fault, that your mother couldn't be there for you in the way you needed her most — as a loving protector. It will free you to feel good instead of guilty for leaving behind your family's unworkable attitudes about women, and it should make it easier to let go of the past as you work toward a better present and future.

You have a right to feel good about yourself as a female and to express it and enjoy it in your own unique way, as long as you don't exploit yourself or others. Sexuality is such a seldom-discussed topic that after an initial quiet period, the women in my sexuality workshops are bursting with things to say and questions to ask. There may be a lot of tears, laughter, and hugs — and nearly everyone is touched in a positive way.

CHAPTER TEN

BUILDING A SUPPORT SYSTEM

BUILDING FRIENDSHIPS WITH OTHER WOMEN

The violation of childhood sexual abuse can shatter the ability of children to trust in their parents, other adult caregivers, and the world in general. It's essential for your recovery that you break out of the isolation imposed by the sexual abuse in your past — to connect with other people and to rebuild your ability to trust. It will be especially helpful if you connect with other women who also have a background of childhood sexual abuse. This can allow you to quit feeling so different from other people.

You need to know there are people who care what happens to you. You need loving and supportive people in your life, friends who can make your life fuller, more enjoyable, and who can help you to deal with your problems. But don't be disappointed if this doesn't happen overnight. It takes work, time, and the willingness to take personal risks.

First of all, I encourage you to work on building up a network of same-sex friends and avoid sexual relationships in the beginning because such relationships may mix in your abuse with caring and friendship. Most women from under-nurturing families — not just those from sexually abusive

113

families — have ambiguous personal boundaries. This affects their ability to say no or to leave an uncomfortable situation. Further, the lack of clearly drawn boundaries almost always exists in their sexual life. This generally makes opposite-sex friendships difficult to handle until later in the recovery process. Until you are fairly secure about your personal boundaries and have developed the strength to enforce them, it's all too easy to have an opposite-sex friendship become sexual because, culturally, women and men relate primarily in a sexual way. The hazard is that a friendship may become sexual against your intentions. Same-sex friendships are not so apt to become sexual because women have learned other ways to connect with each other. It is still important for all women to focus on having friends with no sexual contact involved.

Adult survivors need to set clear sexual boundaries in order to build a safe support system of same-sex friends. Many survivors speak of their fear of being close to anyone. They're afraid being close can turn into being sexual because that's what happened in their family. Be sure to set boundaries that allow you to feel safe and that give you the right to say no if you feel threatened. Clearly defined boundaries make it easier for you to discuss all issues honestly and without feeling threatened.

Intimacy Is *Not* Based on Chaos

Because undernurturing families are usually chaotic, some family members learn to see chaos as a way to connect with each other and unite against a common foe. In the same manner, adult survivors often mistake the chaos and intensity of abusive or hurtful adult relationships for intimacy. This is not intimacy — it's the *illusion* of intimacy.

True intimacy is *not* based on chaos or abuse. True intimacy is feeling connected to another person in times of quiet and peace, as well as in times of stress. It is being able to *trust* that another person cares about you and that you care about him or her. It is something that grows stronger and deeper over time and through being honest. It means sharing life's joys and the sad times too. If people have only learned to connect with others through the intensity of chaos and abuse, they may invent crises and chaos as a way to feel loved and needed. It is an exhausting and a stressful way to relate.

Women may re-create hurtful relationships from their past. Many are told that they are self-destructive. I don't believe that's so. I think we re-create childhood relationships for a number of reasons: (1) it feels familiar, (2) we may not know it can be different or that we deserve a healthy relationship, and (3) many of us will gravitate toward a hurtful situation, friendship, or relationship as a way to make it work out right this time. Meeting caring people and learning new skills can help us prevent re-creating hurtful relationships from our past.

SETTING HEALTHY BOUNDARIES

The easiest way to think of your boundaries is as a set of rules that you write to govern how you allow people to treat you. Abusive family systems teach children that they have no right to set up these boundaries or rules; thus, children may have trouble emotionally emancipating themselves from their families, even if they live across the country. What follows is a list of basic rules that can help you to establish new and healthy boundaries for yourself.

1. Within reason, I have a right to say no to people without feeling guilty — this holds true whether it is my boss, spouse, or even my children. I don't have to let myself be overworked or taken advantage of at home, work, socially, or anywhere else.
2. I will not tolerate abuse. Hitting, slapping, pushing, or physical abuse of any kind is not okay, nor is verbal abuse or other kinds of intimidation. I will not allow another

115

person to force me to be sexual against my will. I have a right to leave if someone is abusive to me.

3. I have a right to privacy. My own things, my journal, my room are mine and people must ask if they want to use anything of mine. I also expect co-workers to ask if they wish to go into my desk and use my equipment.

4. I have a right to expect my friends to support me and do favors for me at times. I'll avoid one-way relationships where I do all the giving.

5. I have a right to be listened to and to share the "air time" with others at home, at work, and in my social circle. I have a right to share only what I want, when I want, and with whom I want.

Begin with these five rules as a basis for building healthy boundaries. As you internalize these rules and solidify the boundaries they create, you will notice feelings of discomfort, anger, and fear when your boundaries are violated. That is how boundaries should function. They are a psychological watchdog to warn you of approaching danger and to help you live the sort of life you want to live. You can fine-tune them any way that fits best for you and add others as you go along. You can also give others the same rights.

BUILDING RELATIONSHIPS

A good way to help build your relationships is to get yourself into a therapy group or other self-help group, or both.

It is important that you understand the concept of boundaries as defined in this chapter. Without healing and rebuilding boundaries, you can't have relationships that are any different from those you had in your abusive family system. It is also important for you to know that if people you are close to are hurting, you don't have to take on their pain and make it your own.

Many adult survivors have had all their family hurts and pains dumped on them. No wonder they find it such a frightening thought to get close to people and thereby choose to avoid intimacy. In their families, being close hurt too much and meant they got stuck holding the bag of destructive emotions. You may have been through this yourself, but remember:

- You are a separate person, even from those you love deeply.
- You have a choice about how you let your feelings affect you. And you also get to choose whether you will let someone else's feelings or remarks affect you.

Let Others Care About You

If you fear being alone and not being dependent on others, it's important that you begin to see yourself as a competent adult. You need to separate the feelings of your inner child, who may now be dominant as a result of your unhealed childhood abuse, from those feelings of your competent adult self.

It may be terrifying for you to think of getting close to others. The fear of more hurt and rejection can be difficult to overcome, but once you quit rejecting yourself you'll find it easier to let others love and care about you. Start telling friends and family members whom you care about how you feel about them. Say "I love you," if that is the way you feel. Fear of separateness and fear of closeness both come from inconsistent parenting and undernurturing.

Take a look at the methods you may use to "protect" yourself — methods that keep people away from you and keep you from having fulfilling relationships.

Do you keep people at bay with your humor, so that others are never sure when you are being serious?

Do you use humor to dismiss any painful feelings you have?

Do you try to be "invisible" by avoiding people at social gatherings?

What about anger? Do you use anger to intimidate people from getting close to you?

Even perfectionism in the way you dress, look, and act can

117

be a way to keep people away. Appearing to be perfect, coupled with an aloof manner, can be very intimidating to others.

As you feel strong enough to get close to people, you can develop healthy personal boundaries. And as you develop boundaries, you'll feel safer to get close to others. You will pay attention to what feels intrusive, what feels supportive, and exactly how much you want to disclose to people when you are asked a question.

Some adult survivors speak of feeling frightened when they are asked questions because they respond almost automatically with personal information, regardless of who asks the question. This type of response indicates weakened boundaries. Stop yourself before responding and ask yourself if you want to answer the question at all. Is the person asking the question someone with whom you're comfortable sharing your feelings? Practice answering questions with responses that allow you to set up boundaries. For example, if someone asks you if you're a Republican or a Democrat, you may want to say, "I don't think that's pertinent to our conversation." Or, "I'm sorry, but I don't like discussing politics except with close friends, and I'm not going to answer your question." As you develop healthy boundaries, you'll be able to say, "No, I choose not to share that information." You'll find that your relationships and friendships are more fun, relaxed, and nurturing.

CHAPTER ELEVEN

CONFRONTING THE OLD FAMILY BLUEPRINT

The way you were treated and what you learned about the world in your childhood family will shape your world view and how you behave with others for your entire life. Later experiences will also affect you, but they will be interpreted through your perception of the world. Unless there is a major change in your life — going through alcohol or other drug abuse treatment, for example — your view of whether people are trustworthy, whether life is fulfilling, and whether you are a worthwhile person won't change much. As an adult survivor, this means you need to make substantial changes in the rules and values (your family blueprint) learned from your family if you are to have a more positive view of the world and your possibilities in it.

Once you understand what the family rules are, you can begin to change the ones that hold you back. Much of your family system was probably hidden, so you may need to work hard at figuring out exactly what your family's attitudes were toward play, work, money, women, sex, and marriage, to really get at the essential values and rules.

The inner core of your belief system consists of all the rules, attitudes, and values that you have learned throughout your life. The strongest elements are those that you learned in your family, but some are from your church, your friends, your schools, and the media. You need to recognize that many of your beliefs may not be in harmony with who you are today. It's very helpful if you make these rules, attitudes, and values, especially those from the family, very clear-cut — that is, write them out. Then you can look at them openly and decide if they are beliefs you want controlling your life. Your beliefs affect all your decisions and relationships. As a survivor of abuse, you have been harboring beliefs that have negatively affected your life and caused you to feel guilt when you tried to do things that were contrary to them.

REWRITING THE RULES

Try making a list of your family rules and add to them as you remember additional ones. In a column next to each rule, write down whether you accept or reject it. Try reading each family rule aloud as you accept it for your own or as you reject or change it. If you reject it, you need to write a rule that refutes it. For example, one of the rules from your family blueprint might be, *When adults get angry, they lose control.* You might want to change it to, *Adults and children can get angry in a responsible manner and work out conflicts in ways that are not abusive to others.* You may experience feelings of anger, sadness, and probably disgust as you uncover some of your family rules.

Once you are aware of your family system and its rules, then you can change the rules to affect the way you relate to others. In group therapy, participants may unconsciously try to re-create the group and its members into some facsimile of their families. They may get into sibling rivalries, see the group leaders as their parents and get jealous about sharing them with others, or worry there isn't enough caring to go around — just as there wasn't in their family.

120

Seeing how your family system gets re-created in group therapy can be very instructive. The group creates a less risky environment to talk about your feelings regarding your family. The knowledge gained in your group can also help you to detach and retain your power when you are around your childhood family.

Fulfillment at Work

Pay attention to your behavior in the workplace. Are you re-creating your old family system with every job? Try to maximize your fulfillment and minimize unnecessary stresses you bring to your job and your relationships with co-workers. Pay particular attention to these questions as they relate to your job:

- *How do you relate to others at work?* Do you feel inferior to those above you? Superior to those who work under you? Or do you feel invisible to everyone, as if you just don't matter?
- *In general, what is your attitude toward bosses?* Are you afraid, hostile? Do you feel valued or fear that you will be discovered for a fraud? Do you resent the boss's power over you? Is it hard to stand up for yourself?
- *Do you see any similarities between your family of origin and how you handle yourself at work?* Are you re-creating your old family system, with victims and abusers, among your workmates?

WRITING YOUR PERSONAL CONSTITUTION

We've already looked at actively challenging and rewriting the rules, attitudes, and values you learned in your under-nurturing family. Now it is time to challenge in more depth the philosophy of life that underlies and comes out of your family belief system.

Writing a *Personal Constitution* or blueprint is a tool that many survivors have found useful to help them expand their philosophy. It encourages them to be active in creating a more positive life philosophy. It can become a written affirmation of you and your life. First, write out, as completely as possible, the rules of your original family system. Then throw out everything you disagree with and replace it with things that are more meaningful and fulfilling to you. There is a relationship between your beliefs and feelings. A negative belief system will make you feel more hopeless, just as a positive one will make you more filled with hope. Betsy's personal constitution is just an example. Your personal constitution will be different, to reflect the things most important to you.

Betsy's Constitution

I, Betsy, am okay just because I am who I am. I do not need to be perfect.

I do not have to prove my worth to anyone.

I have the right to have boundaries and take care of myself.

I have the right to have loving relationships.

I have a right to enjoy my life for me, while respecting myself and others.

I will find time to have fun, to help people and causes I believe in.

My sexuality is a gift; my female body is for me to enjoy, and no one has the right to exploit me.

I will try to make the most of my gift of life, living it in accordance with my beliefs and values.

CONSIDERING RECONCILIATION
WITH YOUR FAMILY

This is a touchy subject with many adult survivors, especially those who are realizing for the first time just how abusive their families really were. This is true whether you were sexually abused in your family or outside of it. Survivors are angry at both the abuser and those who let the abuse take place. I am not saying this anger is out of place. I *am* saying it's important to *consider* reconciliation or having some type of relationship with family. Let's examine the process in more detail.

Reconciliation with your childhood family — including abusers in cases of incest — is a real and distinct possibility. Many of you may be appalled and ask, "How can I possibly reconcile with someone who sexually abused me as a child?" First, you don't have to, and may not want to, reconcile with the abuser, but you may want to reconcile with the rest of your family. Reconciliation doesn't mean that you deny your feelings about the abuse or pretend it never happened. Some survivors make the difficult decision to never see their families again because seeing them would be too painful. But for many there is a middle ground where it is possible to try to work toward acceptance and reconciliation with their families, including or excluding the abuser. They may develop this attitude:

> *Yes, the sexual abuse happened. No, I won't forget it. But I'm willing to accept that it is past, and I refuse to let the memory of it continue to control me through ongoing bitterness and resentment. I would like my family to acknowledge what happened to me and make amends to me in a thoughtful and genuine manner. I'm willing to give reconciliation a try.*

You might be pleasantly surprised at the response of your family — or your attempts may be rebuffed completely. Either way, you come out a winner by taking back your power through initiative and the willingness to talk. Now, let's take a look at how a reconciliation might take place.

Ideally, for most people, the entire family would be *willing* — even if you never ask them or decide not to — to come into the therapeutic situation with you and show a willingness to own up to the abuse and whatever their part in it was. Unfortunately, this is seldom the way things work.

Even when the sexual abuser was not a relative, but was someone known to the family — such as a day-care worker, the son of a family friend, or a clergyman — your family still may deny anything happened to you or may try to minimize it. They either can't stand to look at your pain or don't want to admit that anything they did makes them in any way responsible. They may reject responsibility for having regularly let you be with the abuser or for not noticing that something was wrong. In some ways, any case of ongoing sexual abuse involving a perpetrator known to the family resembles incest in its implications and results, because the abuser was part of the family's social circle or community.

Confronting the Family and the Abuser

Confrontation isn't for everybody, but for some of you, it can be helpful to tell your family about the abuse, and even to confront the abuser when you're ready. I encourage survivors to start with other members of the family, usually siblings, who may be the most supportive. In some cases, it turns out that siblings were also abused. I think, before you speak to your family or confront the abuser, it will be more productive for you to be in a survivors' group before you begin disclosing family secrets to family members, especially if the abuse took place in the immediate family. Know the abuse wasn't your fault; be ready for rejection, and rehearse and role-play the confrontation. Otherwise, you may put high expectations on your family's response and continued support — and you could be disappointed. Family members will have their own shock, pain, denial, and even abuse to deal with. They can't be as detached as people out-side your family can. You generally get more support when your abuser is further removed from your family.

Before you tell family members about your abuse, think about your expectations. Don't set yourself up for the dis-appointment and betrayal you may have felt as a child. Don't expect them to be immediately angry at the abuser. Don't expect them to feel as you do. You have had time to talk and think about your feelings. They have not. Be prepared that they will minimize what you tell them and want you to leave it in the past. Your expectations should be based on what you need *for yourself* — you should not expect others to do anything. You don't have to tell your family anything. Do it only if you want to, and if you feel ready. Here are five positive reasons for telling your family about your abuse:

- You stand up for yourself as a powerful adult.
- You end the secret and silence of the abuse.
- You quit protecting the abuser.
- You stop the abuse cycle and help protect other children.
- You open relationships with supportive family members.

Don't confront an abuser who you fear may be violent or who may try to hurt you. Your safety is important. If you have doubt about the wisdom of a confrontation discuss it with your group or therapist. You can take your power back without directly confronting the abuser, through role-playing and letter writing. If you do decide to confront your abuser directly, *don't expect the abuser to feel sorry.* They are usually defensive and angry that you're bringing it up at all or "mak-ing such a big deal out of it." So make sure you're getting other support. Take time to plan a confrontation carefully; talk to others and do the type of confrontation that feels right for you.

Types of Confrontation

Letter Writing

Start with writing uncensored letters to your abuser about your feelings over the abuse. Let your emotions run high. But don't mail the letters at this point; instead, share them in your group or with a trusted friend. More on letter writing is discussed on pages 127-129.

Face to Face

Talk to your abuser in person. Calmly describe your feelings about the abuse and what you want the abuser to do as a response. For many survivors, hearing the words, "What I did was very wrong, and I am truly sorry for the hurt I've caused you," would be magical. This type of confrontation is usually best done with another person present — for example, your therapist, if you are seeing one — so you don't feel powerless and abused if the abuser becomes angry and abusive toward you.

Going to the Cemetery

Maybe your abuser is dead. If so, going to the cemetery may feel more powerful than writing a letter or having a confrontation with someone role-playing the abuser. Visiting the grave of your abuser and talking about how you feel about the abuse can be a rewarding experience. Again, you may want to spend some time preparing what you want to say.

Legal Action

Some survivors decide they want legal justice for themselves. Take your time before choosing this course of action. You might have to go through a long and complex court case that will not necessarily turn out the way you want it to end. If you do choose legal action, make sure you bring plenty of supportive friends along with you — *don't* go through it alone.

LETTERS TO YOUR FAMILY

Most survivors benefit from writing letters to their abusers and their families. Again, don't mail the first letters you write. Write everything that you have ever wanted to say; don't hold back. This is a chance to express intense feelings about your abuse without worrying about repercussions. Read your letters to your therapist or in a self-help group for abuse survivors and ask for support and feedback. You may write many letters to the same person before feeling you are ready to actually send one.

Some survivors *never* send a letter or talk to family members about their abuse. The choice is yours. The danger here is that if you never share your feelings and tell them what you went through, you may forfeit a chance to feel empowered or connected or close to your family. Letters to your family can allow you to validate your experience, be honest, and open doors for closer and more honest connections with them.

Following are two sample letters:

Letter to Mom

Dear Mom,

I know it's no secret to you that I've tried to keep away from you during the past year. You know why. It's something we all know, but don't talk about. I'm learning that it is important to say it out *loud!* So I'll say it aloud for all the years it was a secret. *Your husband sexually abused me as a little girl!*

I've been remembering how shy and unhappy I was as a child. I remember trying to tell you what was happening and how you got mad and said I was just trying to cause trouble because I didn't like your new husband. I've had nightmares of you going off to work at night when I begged you not to go. You must have wondered what made an eight-year-old child so

127

terrified of being left alone at home with this wonderful new Dad to protect me.

It's so hard for me to be angry at you. I feel guilty because I know now that your life was hard. But I was a *little girl and my life was hard too!* You let me down and even now you aren't there for me. I think I'm afraid to really get mad at you or see you. Maybe I'm afraid I'll feel guilty or maybe it's because I don't know if I can ever forgive you or if you'll ever understand.

I hope some day we can talk about this face to face and I can know that you really do care about me. I want to understand but *damn it, I still want a Mom for that little girl.* I'm discovering how much that still hurts.

Alyce

Letter to Brother as Abuser

Dear Paul,

This letter has been a long time coming. Mom tells me you feel hurt that I didn't talk to you or come to her house for Christmas this year. I really needed some time away from you and the whole family. Everyone acts like I am trying to make you feel bad. No one seems to care at all that I was sexually abused and hurt by you and your friends when I was a little kid. It was *not* experimentation. I get sick of everyone saying that. I was a little girl, and you and your friends were teenagers.

I really looked up to you when we were kids. I liked the attention I got from you because I sure didn't get any from Dad. He was so busy being the big important lawyer around town and acting like he had such a wonderful family. I felt like he took us out only to show us off. You really took advantage of how much I trusted you. I'll never forget the day you called me to come to Brad's house with you and your friends. I felt so happy that I was going to be included with you and all your friends, and even though I felt a little scared, I thought I'd be safe with my big brother!

I continue to have nightmares that people are trying to get me. I am even afraid of me. I don't know if I'll ever even feel safe enough with my husband to be freely sexual with him and *know* I can be safe. It is so scary that the thought that I could ever enjoy it feels alien! I hate you so much for what you did to me and yet, at the same time, I wish I had a big brother. I think that I can't ever be around you again unless you can really understand what happened to me and be truly willing to say you're sorry for what you did — not do it just because that's what Mom would want.

Carol

ASKING THE FAMILY TO THERAPY

Sometimes survivors discuss their abuse with another family member before entering therapy or joining a group — perhaps with a sister who may also have been abused. Most survivors, however, don't have a family ally at the beginning of recovery. If this is so for you, you will need to use the support systems built up in support groups and individual therapy. Nonetheless, bringing any willing family members into a therapy session with you can be a helpful process.

The majority of survivors want some family contact, but some take breaks from their families for months or years. In many cases, it's better to have individual family members come in one at a time. This can decrease the level of denial and make for more open talking. You might want to begin with a sibling or your mom. It is also helpful to get background information from your mom about her own childhood and family. This can help you understand your mom.

Discussing her childhood may also decrease her defensiveness about the session, while heightening her ability to connect with you. It may turn out that Mom — and sometimes Dad — suffered from physical, verbal, or sexual abuse during childhood.

Of course, many families refuse to come in and discuss the abuse. And the abusers usually are the least willing to help.

Any effort toward reconciliation with family members is up to each survivor. Even though the results aren't always what survivors expect, it's still a good idea for them to investigate what help they can get from their families. Sometimes there are many positive and caring feelings and emotions available to survivors from family members.

Some survivors need a break from their family — or at least certain family members — while they do their healing. This can be a good idea, and the survivor can maintain that break until the time feels right to resume contact. When and if you resume contact, you can set the ground rules so you feel safe and in charge of yourself.

If your family is one of the rare cases where some members are dangerously violent and could harm you, I counsel extreme caution. When dealing with violent families, it is best to deal with things on an abstract level. Write letters expressing your feelings — but don't send them. Forget about doing a family therapy session including the violent members and, in general, be careful of any dealings with them. It is still possible for you to deal with the safe family members, but exercise common sense and set well-defined boundaries. It is rare that all members of a family are so dangerous that all contact with them must be severed. In any case, as you learn to set boundaries and take better care of yourself as an adult, the power of your family over you will continue to lessen.

The real prize for talking with your family is breaking the silence and taking back your power, as an adult, from the system that so badly failed you as a child. You can make peace with yourself and your past, whether or not your childhood family is willing to go through the process with you. Remember, if you do have family contact, you have a right to set boundaries and define that contact, leave when it feels abusive, ask for an apology, and even ask that certain family members enter therapy.

CHAPTER TWELVE

GETTING INTO THERAPY

If you have struggled for years with the feelings of pain, inadequacy, and unlovability discussed in this book, two of the best things you can do for yourself are to find a sexual abuse support group and to consider seeing a trained professional, such as a psychologist, social worker, psychiatrist, or counselor. Support specifically in regard to your history of childhood sexual abuse is necessary, even if you are already active in some other type of support group. A good therapist can help you get "unstuck" and provide guidance as you continue your journey of recovery.

Individual therapy or group therapy can speed up your recovery and give you experience and insight in building trusting relationships. For some women, the client and therapist relationship may be the first time they openly discuss the abuse and allow themselves to be so vulnerable to another person. This sort of openness and trust can lay the groundwork for developing close relationships *outside* of therapy.

WHAT TO DO WHEN CHOOSING A THERAPIST

Choosing the right therapist is important. One method is to go to a clinic or to a psychotherapist who is recommended by someone you trust. If you have no recommendation, call a county mental health service, your local women's center, or a rape crisis center for a referral. Your county social services office will usually have its own program or a list of qualified therapists to which you can be referred. When contacting therapists, do not be afraid to ask about their credentials or to ask them to describe their philosophy and type of treatment. It is your right and responsibility to have this information. Credentials of professional therapists should be displayed in their offices or waiting rooms. Trust your intuition and feelings as you interview therapists. If something feels uncomfortable or wrong about certain people, it's probably a good idea not to work with them.

Be sure to ask any therapist you're thinking of working with about the cost of therapy — it can be quite expensive. Check your health insurance policy, if you have one, to see if it includes mental health benefits and how much it covers. Some county programs, and even some private clinics or individual therapists, may be subsidized or otherwise offer some form of a sliding-fee scale based on your ability to pay. That is, the less money you make, the less money you pay for therapy. Chances are that there will be affordable help available to you if you examine all your options.

What to Look for in a Therapist

I am often asked what I think of female adult survivors of childhood sexual abuse working with male therapists. It is important to define your needs. Generally, I think it is easier and more helpful for women who have been sexually abused to begin their therapy by connecting with a therapist of their same sex. A woman severely abused by her mom may feel safer seeing a male therapist. Some lesbian women feel strongly about seeing a lesbian therapist. Basically, I believe women can connect and relate more to the dynamics of female abuse than a male can. I have worked with men severely abused by their dads who were too afraid to be vulnerable with a male authority figure as a therapist. After they have been in therapy for a time, however, I ask them to see a male therapist because I can't give them the personal male understanding. One of the first tasks in therapy is to begin building a support system of same-sex friends, and a same-sex therapist will better start that process for you.

It is important that you work with a therapist experienced in working with sexual abuse clients, with solid, respectful boundaries regarding clients. That means the therapist listens to what you say and doesn't tell you how you feel. Instead, the therapist lets you proceed at your own pace and comfort level, pointing you in the right directions without pushing you into discussing topics you aren't ready to talk about. Be wary of a therapist who does a lot of physical touching and holding in sessions. You'll know when it feels okay to get or give a hug. In general, you should listen to your inner voice regarding therapy. If you consistently feel that working with a certain therapist feels wrong and that you are not getting what you want out of therapy, it's probably a good idea to look elsewhere for help.

Be Wary of the Wrong Type of Therapy

If a therapist is pushy and not respectful of your pace, you may end up re-creating some of the abusive dynamics that existed in your childhood family. Be wary of therapies that reenact your abuse or push you to have total recall through hypnosis or psychodrama — there is a possibility that you will be retraumatized by such actions.

WHAT HAPPENS IN THERAPY?

Here's how a therapist might work with you as a new client: She will begin by taking a family history to give her a frame of reference. The problems you come to therapy for are the basis of what you will explore. The therapist will ask you to look at how you think and feel about the problems at the present moment, how they affect you, and what you think you can do to change things. Problems may be anything that you feel stuck about or want an outside opinion on. They can be secrets that have been painful to carry alone — guilt over the abuse, marriage problems, depression or hopelessness, feeling lonely or inadequate — or just about anything under the sun.

You will discuss what you want your goals in therapy to be. She will tell you how she usually works with clients, and some of the "homework" she might ask you to do. You might discuss the approximate length of your therapy. And even though the total length of time might seem long, you should realize that by deciding on therapy and being honest with yourself, you may begin feeling some relief after your initial sessions.

When they are ready, I refer almost 100 percent of the women who come to me for help to some sort of group in addition to the individual therapy. I really believe that what survivors need the most is to build a support system, and the sooner they begin, the better. Most people who come for therapy *do* have a few friends, but many don't have close friends with whom they feel they can totally be themselves and still be accepted.

Many women new to therapy say they feel a wave of relief from telling their therapist long-held secrets and getting an affirming, nonjudgmental response. After this initial relief, they may go through a period of remorse or feeling worse for a while as they come to grips with the reality of having broken their family rule of "not talking" by remembering and disclosing the painful events from their childhoods to ''an outsider.'' Discussing the childhood events may provoke some strong feelings they were never allowed to have in their families. In many cases it can strongly affect relationships with their childhood families for a long time. Therapy will be most effective when it deals with healing the past and relating it to the present so you can live more actively and contentedly.

Recovering survivors may feel distant, angry, hurt, and mistrustful around other family members. These are normal feelings, and they will settle down after awhile. Often, parents and siblings can't be very supportive to the survivors unless they are also getting some help. Families may still be in denial about the sexual abuse, or simply feel too afraid of talking or thinking about it.

Some women may not feel like being sexual for a period of time. Others, already feeling ''defective'' sexually from their history of abuse, may feel *less* shame and stress around their sexuality. Now they have permission to feel or not to feel sexual, without feeling guilty. Each of us has our own recovery process, although there are some common stages of therapy.

Stages of Therapy

1. *Recognition.* This is admitting to yourself that something happened. This may occur when you seek help.
2. *Breaking the Silence.* This entails talking about abuse, maybe for the first time. It begins to end the secrets and isolation.
3. *Connecting with Others.* As you connect with others who are respectful, they believe you and validate your reality. You are not crazy. The abuse was wrong, and it was scary and did hurt you. Each encounter with those who support you will build your trust.
4. *Grieving.* This is expressing feelings of grief, anger, fear, sadness, denial, and shock for your losses. Grieving will allow for more and more healing and acceptance.

5. *Renewal.* This is the stage where you get energized from your grief process. It's like spring after winter, and it's a very empowering and creative stage.

The stages can be seen as circular because we go back to stage one as we recognize another piece from our past or tell a new person about our abuse. Each time we recycle the stages, we come through with a deeper healing, more peace, and more energy.

Transference

Your childhood family's rules and bonds are very strong and you learned them at a very early age, so it's not surprising if you describe people in your life by relating them back to your childhood family. Your husband may seem "just like my dad," or a friend may be acting "just like my sister or mother." This kind of labeling is called *transference* and may not be fair to the people you are labeling. They may be offended by your constant comparisons. Not making comparisons will enable you to keep your current relationships separate from unresolved feelings toward members of your childhood family. Let your significant others know some of what you are working on in therapy so they can better understand the recovery process and not feel left out.

Adult survivors tend to see the world treating them in unloving ways and may distort some of what is happening to them to fit in with old abusive family belief systems. This is another case of negative transference. If something seems abusive to you, then ask the people involved, especially those you trust, to clarify things for you. Be aware of the possibility that you may unconsciously distort some things because of your abuse background.

JOINING A GROUP

One of the best and most constructive ways for someone to take a big leap forward on the road to recovery from childhood sexual abuse is to join a therapy group specifically for abuse survivors. Group therapy for adult survivors offers the safety factors of a professionally trained group facilitator and a highly structured setting. Groups have rules that protect all members. Some survivors want the structured support and feedback such groups provide to help them get through frightening feelings. Being in this sort of group can re-create some of the positive family dynamics that members missed in their growing up years. It's a chance to experience what it is like in a safe family environment where family members are respected and protected — no abusive behavior is allowed in these groups, and you are encouraged to discuss your feelings.

It's helpful when people can say they feel jealous or competitive, without fearing they will be shouted down. You can talk about how your childhood family operated and almost always find other group members who understand and sympathize. Whether physical touch was used to hurt you as a child or if you suffered from an almost total lack of touching and nurturing, safe touching is very healing. Therapy groups can be a great place to give and receive caring touches and hugs.

Self-help groups such as Incest Anonymous or Sexual Abuse Anonymous are based on the Twelve Steps originated by the founders of Alcoholics Anonymous. These Steps are a blueprint for a better way of life. Within such groups, you can find hope, connect with others, find a spiritual path acceptable to your philosophy, and come to accept and care for yourself as a worthwhile person. These groups are readily available all over the country. Joining one is not a prerequisite for recovery, but it is a loving, accessible place to start.

The combination of working with a good, understanding therapist in individual counseling and joining a group of like-minded adult survivors sharing their recovery is almost unbeatable. I strongly urge you to try both.

EMERGING FROM YOUR COCOON

You are beginning a transformation, even if you are just beginning to openly work on your childhood sexual abuse issues. Keep talking to people you trust, keep a journal, join a group, see a therapist, read books on the subject, and trust yourself. The more work you do, the stronger your healing is bound to be. You have many resources available to you, in addition to your personal strengths and courage. Use them all. Trust yourself enough to believe that you will find the answers you need, as long as you are willing to work hard. Many others have transformed themselves before you. The answers are there for everybody. There is enough recovery to go around for all of you.

It may take a long time, but day by day you will gradually emerge from the burden of pain and shame caused by your past. Through understanding what happened to you, you will be able to accept that you are blameless regarding the childhood abuse you suffered, and you will learn to affirm your own sense of self-worth by connecting with other people in healthy ways.

You can't change the past, but you can understand it, and you can make friends with it as much as possible. You can empower yourself by learning what you missed and striving to put it back into your life. You can do this through connecting with other people; through putting aside your old negative beliefs and replacing them with positive ones; through learning to love and cherish the innocent child that you were.

So go slowly and ask for help along the way, and know that you will never again allow yourself to be a victim of abuse. Healing means having loving relationships and appreciating who and what you are. It is the freedom to enjoy being yourself. Take flight on your new wings.

RESOURCES
Help for Sexual Abuse Survivors

INCEST SURVIVORS ANONYMOUS
P.O. Box 5613
Long Beach, CA 90805-0613

Advocacy work and referrals:
NATIONAL ORGANIZATION FOR VICTIM ASSISTANCE
(NOVA)
717 D Street N.W.
Suite 200
Washington DC 20004
1-202-939-NOVA

Counseling for survivors and families:
AMACU (Adults Molested as Children)
c/o Parents United
P.O. Box 952
San Jose, CA 95108
1-408-280-5055

A forum for survivors to share their thoughts and arts with others:
INCEST SURVIVOR INFORMATION EXCHANGE
P.O. Box 3399
New Haven, CT 06515

You can find help from local self-help groups and from psychotherapists for sexual abuse survivors through your region women's centers, sexual assault centers, and county social services.

SUGGESTED READING

Women who have a history of childhood sexual abuse have special areas about which they may want more in-depth information. Below is a listing of books that cover such topics as addiction, child abuse, intimacy, parenting, sexual abuse, and shame. The list is not comprehensive, but it will give you a starting point for gathering more information.

Alcoholics Anonymous. Third Edition. New York: Alcoholics Anonymous World Services, Inc., 1976.

Barbach, Lonnie. *For Yourself: The Fulfillment of Female Sexuality.* Garden City, N. Y.: Anchor Books, 1976.

Bass, Ellen, and Laura Davis. *The Courage to Heal.* New York: Harper & Row, 1988.

Beattie, Melody. *Codependent No More.* Center City, Minn.: Hazelden Educational Materials, 1987.

Black, Claudia. *It Will Never Happen to Me!* Denver: M.A.C., 1982.

Butler, Sandra. *Conspiracy of Silence: The Trauma of Incest.* San Francisco: Volcano Press, 1985.

Carnes, Patrick. *The Sexual Addiction.* Minneapolis: CompCare Publications, 1983.

Clarke, Jean Illsley. *Self Esteem: A Family Affair.* Minneapolis: Winston Press, 1979.

Clarke, Jean Illsley, and Connie Dawson. *Growing Up Again: Parenting Ourselves, Parenting Our Children.* Center City, Minn.: Hazelden Educational Materials, 1989.

Each Day a New Beginning. Center City, Minn.: Hazelden Educational Materials, 1982.

Finkelhor, David. *Sexually Victimized Children.* New York: Free Press, 1979.

Forward, Susan, and Craig Buck. *Betrayal of Innocence.* New York: Penguin, 1978.

Fossum, Merle, and Marilyn Mason. *Facing Shame.* New York: W. W. Norton, 1986.

Gil, Eliana. *Outgrowing the Pain.* San Francisco: Launch Press, 1983.

Herman, Judith. *Father-Daughter Incest.* Cambridge, Mass.: Harvard University Press, 1982.

Kaufman, Gershen, and Lev Raphael. *The Dynamics of Power: Building a Competent Self.* Cambridge, Mass.: Schenkman Publishing, 1983.

Larsen, Earnie. *Stage II Recovery: Life Beyond Addiction.* San Francisco: Harper & Row, 1985.

Loulan, JoAnn. *Lesbian Sex.* San Francisco: Spinsters Aunt Lute, 1984.

Maltz, Wendy, and Beverly Holman. *Incest and Sexuality.* Lexington, Mass.: Lexington Books, 1987.

Miller, Alice. *For Your Own Good: Hidden Cruelty in Child Rearing and the Roots of Violence.* New York: Farrar, Straus & Giroux, 1980.

Nakken, Craig. *The Addictive Personality: Roots, Rituals, and Recovery.* Center City, Minn.: Hazelden Educational Materials, 1988.

Norwood, Robin. *Women Who Love Too Much.* New York: Jeremy Tarcher, 1985.

Rush, Florence. *The Best Kept Secret: Sexual Abuse of Children.* Englewood Cliffs, N.J.: Prentice Hall, 1980.

Russell, Diana. *The Secret Trauma: Incest in the Lives of Girls and Women.* New York: Basic Books, 1986.

Whitfield, Charles. *Healing the Child Within.* Pompano Beach, Fla: Health Communications, 1988.

INDEX

V
Verbal abuse, 29, 89
Vigilant parent, 57

W
Women for Sobriety, 77
Workplace, behavior in, 121

Other titles that will interest you. . .

Letting Go of Shame
Understanding How Shame Affects Your Life
by Ronald Potter-Efron and Patricia Potter-Efron

This book offers survivors of childhood sexual abuse support for accepting themselves and coping with feelings of shame. It includes a personalized plan of action to build self-esteem and let go of shame. Practical exercises guide us through the process of understanding and taking positive action when our shame threatens to disconnect us from others and ourselves. 192 pp.
Order No. 5082

Of Course You're Angry
by Gayle Rosellini and Mark Worden

Feeling angry is both normal and healthy. Yet learning to express anger appropriately is difficult for those experiencing the fear, guilt, and unpredictability that exists in families recovering from chemical dependency or other dysfunctional behavior. This book looks at various expressions of anger such as violence, depression, and manipulation, and offers specific guidelines for learning healthy ways to acknowledge and express anger. 92 pp.
Order No. 1169

For price and order information, please call one of our Telephone Representatives. Ask for a free catalog describing more than 1,500 items available through Hazelden Educational Materials.

HAZELDEN EDUCATIONAL MATERIALS

1-800-328-9000   **1-800-257-0070**   **1-612-257-4010**
(Toll Free. U.S. Only)   (Toll Free. MN Only)   (AK and Outside U.S.)

Pleasant Valley Road • P.O. Box 176 • Center City, MN 55012-0176